Palgrave Studies in Classical Liberalism

Series Editors

David F. Hardwick, Department of Pathology and Laboratory Medicine, The University of British Columbia, Vancouver, Canada

Leslie Marsh, Department of Economics, Philosophy and Political Science, The University of British Columbia, Okanagan, Canada

This series offers a forum to writers concerned that the central presuppositions of the liberal tradition have been severely corroded, neglected, or misappropriated by overly rationalistic and constructivist approaches.

The hardest-won achievement of the liberal tradition has been the wrestling of epistemic independence from overwhelming concentrations of power, monopolies and capricious zealotries. The very precondition of knowledge is the exploitation of the epistemic virtues accorded by society's situated and distributed manifold of spontaneous orders, the DNA of the modern civil condition.

With the confluence of interest in situated and distributed liberalism emanating from the Scottish tradition, Austrian and behavioral economics, non-Cartesian philosophy and moral psychology, the editors are soliciting proposals that speak to this multidisciplinary constituency. Sole or joint authorship submissions are welcome as are edited collections, broadly theoretical or topical in nature.

Christopher Adair-Toteff

Schmitt on Sovereignty and the State of Exception

A Commentary on Carl Schmitt's 'Politische Theologie'

Christopher Adair-Toteff
Charlottesville, VA, USA

ISSN 2662-6470   ISSN 2662-6489   (electronic)
Palgrave Studies in Classical Liberalism
ISBN 978-3-031-91727-1   ISBN 978-3-031-91728-8   (eBook)
https://doi.org/10.1007/978-3-031-91728-8

Cover credit: © Harvey Loake

This Palgrave Macmillan imprint is published by the registered company Springer Nature Switzerland AG
The registered company address is: Gewerbestrasse 11, 6330 Cham, Switzerland

If disposing of this product, please recycle the paper.

Competing Interests The author has no competing interests to declare that are relevant to the content of this manuscript.

CONTENTS

CHAPTER 1

Carl Schmitt's "Sovereignty": An Introduction

Abstract This chapter introduces Carl Schmitt's conception of sovereignty and locates it within the context of his *Politische Theologie* (1922). It emphasizes the fact that while many commentators have tended to focus on Schmitt's notion of "political theology," his own emphasis was on the concept of sovereignty. That is made clear by the subtitle that he chose and by the title that he used in the three chapters which he contributed to Melchior Palyi's 1923 two-volume collection dedicated to Max Weber's memory. The chapter contains chapter overviews and provides clarification and comments about Schmitt's sources.

Keywords Sovereignty · Ausnahmezustand · Carl Schmitt · Exception · Decision

Carl Schmitt began his work on sovereignty with the sentence "Souverän ist, wer über den Ausnahmezustand entscheidet" (Schmitt, 1934: 11). This can be translated as "The sovereign is the one who decides over the state of exception." This sentence is one of Schmitt's best-known sentences and reflects one of his most important contributions to political theory. But, unlike Schmitt's other equally famous conception of the

© The Author(s), under exclusive license to Springer Nature Switzerland AG 2025
C. Adair-Toteff, *Schmitt on Sovereignty and the State of Exception*, Palgrave Studies in Classical Liberalism, https://doi.org/10.1007/978-3-031-91728-8_1

"Freund-Feind" ("friend-enemy") distinction, the sovereignty sentence is not easily understandable.[1] There are numerous reasons for this and it is the purpose of this slim volume to explain what Schmitt meant by that sentence. In effect, this book is intended to be an in-depth analysis of Carl Schmitt's 1922 book *Politische Theologie*. While commentators have focused on the phrase "political theology," Schmitt made it very clear that the book was devoted to the doctrine of sovereignty. Of the four chapters, one is on state philosophy (IV), one is on political theology (III), but two are devoted to sovereignty (I and II). The emphasis on sovereignty is why Schmitt gave *Politische Theologie* the subtitle *Vier Kapitel zur Lehre von der Souveränität (Four Chapters on the Doctrine of Sovereignty)*. It is also why he chose the title "Soziologie des Souveränitätsbegriffes und politische Theologie" for his contribution to the two-volume work in honor of Max Weber. It is also why Schmitt regarded himself as the last thinker to be concerned with the concept of sovereignty and why he regarded himself as the "brother" to the first two major proponents of the doctrine of sovereignty: Jean Bodin and Thomas Hobbes.

The remainder of this first chapter is divided into four sections. The first section provides a brief history of Schmitt's writings prior to *Politische Theologie* and offers a philosophical-legal context for his decisionism. The second section contains a discussion of Schmitt's concept of sovereignty in its specific context and that means exploring the different editions and noting the significant changes. Carl Schmitt was well-known for not clearly expressing his ideas and for often revising his thoughts; yet, his ideas regarding authority and sovereignty tended to remain the same throughout his life. But this book is not about Schmitt's complete life but is restricted to being a "commentary" on one of his early works.[2]

---

[1] For Schmitt's distinction between "Freund und Feind" see *Der Begriff des Politischen* (Schmitt, 1932: 46–48, 2015b: 60–62). Ernst-Wolfgang Böckenförde famously argued that the concept of the political is the key to Carl Schmitt's "staatsrechtliche" work (Böckenförde, 1988: 283, 286–287). He insisted that the key issue was "unity" ("Einheit"), There is no doubt that Schmitt was often concerned with "Einheit" and one means of bolstering that sense was to set Germany against others. That was one way of interpreting his "Freund-Feind" distinction.

[2] A reader might find it puzzling to have a book-length "commentary" on a rather small work—one that appeared as a fifty-some page book and as a chapter in a collection. But philosophers have sometimes written commentaries that were far larger than the work the commentator was writing on. To offer two instructive examples, Hans Vaihinger published the first volume of his *Kommentar zu Kants Kritik der reinen Vernuft* in 1881 and the second volume in 1892. The total pages of both volumes is close to 1070 pages and they

The third section is composed of brief overviews of the chapters. The fourth section contains some comments of clarification as well as a note about sources.

CARL SCHMITT 1912–1922

Carl Schmitt (1888–1985) counts as one of the most controversial legal philosophers of the twentieth century. In a letter that his biographer Reinhard Mehring cites, Schmitt wrote that that he was born in Plattenberg (Westfalen), studied at Berlin, München, and Straßburg and "habilitated" there in 1914. From 1921 to 1945 he was full professor for public law at Greifswald, Bonn, Köln, and Berlin. After the war, he lost his teaching position and from 1947 he lived in Plattenberg. He listed three of his books: *Die Diktatur* (1921), *Verfassungslehre* (1928), and *Der Nomos* (1950) (Mehring, 2009: 13). This letter provided only the briefest indication of who Schmitt was and what he had accomplished. But, at the time he wrote *Politische Theologie* he was only at the beginning of his academic career and in establishing his reputation. His life was always complex but the years 1910 to 1922 were difficult for professional and personal reasons. It was difficult professionally because of the First World War and its revolutionary aftermath. Schmitt had earned his degree at Straßburg in 1910 and on the basis of another work was licensed to teach at the university level in 1916. His *Gesetz und Urteil (Law and Judgment)* (1912) has been mostly neglected with some justification.[3] It is an earlier work and it reflected the views of his mentor—Fritz van Calker. His third major work was more promising: *Der Wert des Staates und die Bedeutung des Einzelnen (The Value of the State and the Significance of*

cover just the first fifty pages of Kant's first *Kritik* (Vaihinger, 1881, 1892). He never completed it because of eyesight problems. The second example is Joseph Owen's *The Doctrine of Being in the Aristotelian Metaphysics*. This work is a commentary on just the notion of "Being" in the *Metaphysics* and is 539 pages in length (Owens, 1978). This is not to suggest that this is the proper approach to take in general, but I believe that it was certainly warranted in the cases of Aristotle and Kant. I would not presume to place Carl Schmitt alongside those great philosophers, yet I contend that Schmitt's doctrine of sovereignty warrants a brief "commentary."

[3] *Gesetz und Urteil* has a subtitle: *Eine Untersuchung zum Problem der Rechtspraxis (An Investigation into a Problem of Legal Practice)*. Its greatest strength comes in the fourth and final chapter which focused on the problem of making the right judgment (Schmitt, 1969: 68–114).

the Individuals) (1914) because he discussed the relationship between law and power (Neuman, 2015: 16–22). The war years were particularly troubling for Schmitt. He was serving in München and he seemed bored with his military duties and bored with life (Neuman, 2015: 6–8). He thought about suicide but continued to work and to write (Schmitt, 2005: 23–24, 49, 55, 63, 83, 120, 125, 148–149; Mehring, 2009: 88, 110–111). Most of these pieces are articles but the notion of the "state of exception" ("Ausnahmezustand") appears with increasing frequency. But that was only one theme among several. In 1919 Schmitt published *Politische Romantik* in which he criticized the Romantics' emphasis on individuality and its subjectivity. The "state of exception" is the dominate idea of his 1921 book on the nature of dictatorship. *Die Diktatur* is the work that brought Carl Schmitt the most attention thus far, and the beginning of his notoriety (Mehring, 2009: 118–123). His personal life appeared to have stabilized and even improved when he married Pawla (Pauline) Dorotić. For a year his published writings carried the name Schmitt-Dorotić which, as Schmitt's earlier biographer had noted, indicated that he was rather proud of her. But Paul Noack explained that Pauline was a fraud; rather than being a Slavic noble she was a daughter of a Viennese tailor (Noack, 1993: 42–46). Carl Schmitt continued to have professional difficulties and personal crises for most of his life. But his second marriage (to Duška) and his appointment to Bonn and then Berlin marked turning points to a better life—but these things happened after 1922 and his work on sovereignty.

SCHMITT ON SOVEREIGNTY

When Carl Schmitt published *Politische Theologie* in 1922, he had established himself as a major scholar having published *Gesetz und Urteil* in 1912, *Politische Romantik* in 1919, and *Die Diktatur* in 1921. In 1922 he was appointed as full professor ("Ordentliche Professur") at Bonn as the successor to Rudolf Smend who moved to Berlin (Mehring, 1992: 37–38, 187, 2009: 123, 141). In his biography of Carl Schmitt, Mehring explained that Schmitt was chosen to contribute to the Weber *Erinnerungsgabe* partially because of Schmitt's friendship with Melchoir Palyi and partially because of Schmitt's participation in Weber's final seminar on the sociology of the state (Mehring, 2009: 124–125; Weber, 2009: 50). Mehring maintained that Schmitt wrote the fourth chapter "Zur Staatsphilosophie der Gegenrevolution" earlier and that the first three chapters were Schmitt's answer to Weber's concept of "Herrschaft." Weber had insisted that the mark of the state was that it possessed the monopoly on physical force (Weber, 2009: 74). In his 1919 lecture "Politik als Beruf" Weber had made this even clearer when he defined the state as having "das *Monopol legitimer physischer Gewaltsamkeit*" ("the *monopoly of legitimate physical force*") (Weber, 1994: 159). Weber placed emphasis on obedience and that is why he provided his three-fold account of "Herrschaft." People obeyed because of tradition, because of legal rules, or because of personal charisma. Schmitt took issue with that because it did not focus on the person who makes decisions and because it overlooks the importance of sovereignty. In "Politik als Beruf" the concept of sovereignty is missing; in "Staatssoziologie" it is mentioned only in passing (Weber, 2009: 68). Yet, it is clear from the opening sentence of the essay and the book that Schmitt regarded the concept of sovereignty as "the doctrine" of the state. Whether one accepts Mehring's claim that Schmitt's *Politische Theologie* is a response to Weber's work on "Herrschaft" can be debated; what cannot be questioned is Schmitt's insistence on sovereignty and the need for the sovereign to decide the exceptional cases.

Chapter Overviews

Chapter 2: In 1950 Schmitt published *Ex Captivitate Salus* in which he gave an account of the two times he was incarcerated by the Americans. Much of this book is depressing and not all that enlightening; however, there is one notable section that is highly revealing about how Schmitt viewed himself and his connection to law. In this section Schmitt maintained that the two "founders" of the modern theory of law, Jean Bodin and Thomas Hobbes, were basically like brothers to him. They shared the same need for order in the face of chaos; they both believed that law was based upon a sovereign. They all believed that the state needs a strong and decisive leader in order to survive. This chapter also included an examination of the doctrines of sovereignty that are found in the writings by Bodin and Hobbes and shows how much Schmitt relied on Bodin and Hobbes for his own theory of sovereignty in *Politische Theologie* and how much de departed from it.

Chapter 3: There are many ideas in Schmitt's *Politische Theologie*. The book's title and subtitle indicate that the topics which he covers in this book include politics and theology as well as law, philosophy, and theology. The sheer breadth of Schmitt's learning is daunting enough.

However, many scholars read his books as if they were normal works written by normal scholars. Schmitt's writings are not typical nor was Schmitt a typical author. He was always interested in the abnormal, the exceptional, and the unusual, and one understands his ideas better when one has a better understanding of Schmitt as a person. Schmitt's works are highly personal; what he experienced in life is often transferred into words. Schmitt also regarded life as a conflict and he frequently considered his critics to be enemies. This was certainly true regarding Hans Kelsen. It is Kelsen who is frequently attacked in Schmitt's works, but there are others as well in *Politische Theologie*. Schmitt often accused others of not providing answers and being too polemical. *Politische Theologie* is a polemical work and while it is ostensibly about "political theology" he does not really provide a definition of what that is.

Chapter 4: Chapter I of *Politische Theologie* was focused on providing a definition of sovereignty and on offering a history of the concept. Chapter II concentrates on solving problems regarding sovereignty and in confronting Schmitt's contemporaries. The chapter's title reflects the attempt to find a definition of sovereignty while the chapter's contents indicate the history of the concept. The title can be translated as "The Problem of Sovereignty as the Problem of Legal Form and the Decision" ("Das Problem der Souveränität als Problem der Rechtsform und der Entscheidung") (Schmitt, 1923: 11, 1934: 23, 2015a: 23). Schmitt references a large number of individuals but concentrates on only a few scholars. He focuses particularly on Hans Kelsen and Hugo Krabbe but also on Kurt Wolzendorff. With the exceptions of Bodin and Hobbes, most of the scholars that Schmitt was criticizing in this chapter had published their works within the previous decade. Furthermore, Schmitt held Bodin and Hobbes in high regard; he was highly critical of his contemporaries.

Chapter 5: In Chapter III Carl Schmitt begins to lay out his positive theory, but even here much of it is negative and critical. He accuses many legal scholars from the nineteenth and twentieth centuries of being polemical. Yet, a similar complaint might be said about Schmitt regarding the two previous chapters as well as the one now under examination. Schmitt's target is again mainly Hans Kelsen, but Hugo Krabbe and Hugo Preuß are also criticized. Even Max Weber's sociology of the state is found to be defective. In each of these cases, the scholar has committed a cardinal offense; that is, to eliminate theology from law. This is a cardinal offense for two reasons: it obscures the history of legal thinking and it distorts the nature of law. Schmitt adds another discipline to the two he has already addressed and that is philosophy. Whereas the first two chapters were focused on law and sociology; Chapter III includes those to and adds philosophy and theology. Schmitt mentions Hobbes again, but he also includes René Descartes, Gottfried Wilhelm Leibniz, and Jean-Jacques Rousseau. Despite the introduction of theology and philosophy, politics is lurking in the background. Hence, Schmitt's Chapter 3 has the title "Politische Theologie."

Chapter 6: Carl Schmitt's Chapter 4 differs from the previous in at least two substantial ways. First, it has little to do with sovereignty and almost nothing to do with sociology. That may be why Schmitt chose not to include it in the version found in the volume in honor of Max Weber. Second, while Chapter 4 does discuss the importance of decisions, that concept is frequently obscured by Schmitt's discussions of some counter-revolutionaries, his insistence on the need for a dictator, and the modern emphasis on economics. These two reasons account for the slightly truncated discussion of Chapter 4.

The title of Chapter 4 indicates that it is not really about sovereignty and it has nothing to do with sociology. Instead, it is about the philosophy of the state as embodied in the thinking of the counter revolution ("Zur Staatsphilosophie der Gegenrevolution"). Donoso Cortés is mentioned in the subtitle as are De Maistre and Bonald. Schmitt denounces democracy because it leads to eternal discussions and he praises authoritarianism because its leaders are decisive. Decisions, not discussions can be regarded as the theme of this chapter. Unlike the previous three chapters, Chapter 4 does not have many connections to the others and can be read as a self-standing essay.

Chapter 7: This chapter is more than just a simple summary or a brief conclusion; instead, it also considers Schmitt's concept of sovereignty and his notion of "political theology. This concluding chapter has three parts. The first concerns the continual interest in the nature and function of political theology and it focuses on a number of recent books which either are devoted to the topic or are reflections on Schmitt's book. The second part focuses on the notion of sovereignty, not as a general concept, but as a reflection of Schmitt's concept as set out in *Politische Theologie*. Here, the concern is with a few books but also with articles and chapters. Taken together, these two parts provide an indication of Carl Schmitt's lasting influence on legal philosophy and political thinking. The third part is devoted to allowing Schmitt to have the final word. This is found in his

Politische Theologie II. Published almost more than a half century after *Politische Theologie, Politische Theologie II* provides an intriguing look at how Schmitt's understanding of the connection between law, politics, and theology had changed and what he thought might be some of the lasting ideas from his conception of "political theology."

FINAL COMMENTS

These final comments are intended to clarify and correct some claims that I made in *Carl Schmitt on Law and Liberalism*. At the time I was writing that book I understood the importance of Hobbes in Schmitt's thinking about sovereignty, but I had not fully appreciated how crucial Bodin's concept of sovereignty was to Schmitt's thinking. I think I was correct in suggesting that the title of Schmitt's contribution to the Palyi collection was chosen to make it appear more suitable to fit in a collection in sociology. But for the most part Schmitt dismissed sociology as a discipline, but it was clear that he held Weber in high regard. What I did not sufficiently appreciate was how crucial the concept of sovereignty was to Schmitt's thinking at the time and how later he regarded himself as the heir and "brother" to Bodin and Hobbes.[4] Finally, I acknowledge the mistake in the publication of Schmitt's essay and *Politische Theologie*. The book appeared in 1922 and the essay the following year.[5]

Carl Schmitt does not have the status of either Kant or Hegel; his reputation does not even match that of Max Weber. Regardless of what one thinks of Schmitt's political views, one has to acknowledge that he was one of the most important jurists of the twentieth century. And, one must admit that his conception of sovereignty continues to have relevance. It has relevance because these first decades of the twenty-first century have, as with those of the first decades of the twentieth, been ones of crises and conflicts. Reinhard Mehring was correct to insist that "Schmitts Leben war eine Krisenbiographie." ("Schmitt's life was a crisis

---

[4] Even Schmitt experts such as Reinhard Mehring have tended to overlook Bodin's influence on Schmitt's doctrine of sovereignty. Bodin is not mentioned in Mehring's (2014) collection nor in his 1992 short biography. Bodin is mentioned briefly three times in Mehring's (2009) biography (Mehring, 2009: 118, 406, and 446).

[5] There is a discrepancy regarding the time in which Schmitt wrote the piece and when it was published. Mehring wrote that Schmitt composed Chapter IV "during the summer 1922" ("im Sommer 1922") but in the "Vorbemerkung zur Zweiten Ausgabe" he wrote that it was published in March 1922 (Mehring, 2009: 124, Schmitt, 2015a: 7).

biography.") (Mehring, 2014: 6). According to Schmitt, in times of crises, it is insufficient to debate; it is imperative to decide. It is the sovereign who must decide during a "state of exception" ("Ausnahmezustand").

A Note on Schmitt's Sources

As with many of his contemporaries, Carl Schmitt was often careless in citing his sources. Often, he would simply neglect to provide more than an individual's name. He rarely provided a full title of a work that he was using, and the details that he did provide were not always correct. I have attempted to determine what work Schmitt was referring to but I have occasionally not been successful. Sometimes I have thought that Schmitt did not really care whether he provided citations; other times, other times I have believed that he omitted any information that would prove his interpretation to be mistaken. Schmitt was highly effective as a partisan politician; as an impartial scholar (in the Weberian sense), he was not always successful. As a scholarly work, *Politische Theologie* leaves much to be desires; but as a political work, it is impressive and has lasting importance.

References

Adair-Toteff, C. (2020). *Carl Schmitt on Law and Liberalism*. Palgrave/ Macmillan.

Böckenförde, E-W. (1988). Der Begriff des Politischen als Schlüssel zum Staatsrechtlichen Werk Carl Schmitts. In *Complexio Oppositorum. Über Carl Schmitt* (pp. 289–305). Herausgegeben von Helmut Quaritsch. Duncker & Humblot.

Mehring, R. (2014). *Kriegstechniker des Begriffs. Biographische Studien zu Carl Schmitt*. Mohr Siebeck.

Mehring, R. (2009). *Carl Schmitt. Aufstieg und Fall. Eine Biographie*. Verlag C.H. Beck.

Mehring, R. (1992). *Carl Schmitt zur Einführung*. Junius.

Neumann, V. (2015). *Carl Schmitt als Jurist*. Mohr Siebeck.

Owens, J. (1978). *The Doctrine of Being in the Aristotelian Metaphysics* (3rd Edn). Pontifical Institute of Medieval Studies.

Schmitt, C. (2015a). *Politische Theologie. Vier Kapitel zur Lehre von der Souveränität*. Duncker & Humblot. Zehnte Auflage.

Schmitt, C. (2015b). *Der Begriff des Politischen. Text von 1932 mit einem Vorwort und drei Corollarien*. Duncker & Humblot. 9., korrigierte Auflage.

Schmitt, C. (2015c). *Ex Captivitate Salus. Erfahrungen der Zeit 1945/47*. Duncker & Humblot. Vierte, erweiterte Aufllage.

Schmitt, C. (2005). *Carl Schmitt. Die Militärzeit 1915 bis 1919. Tagebuch Februar bis Dezember 1915. Aufsätze und Materiallen*. Herausgegeben von Ernst Hüsmert und Gerd Giesler. Akademie Verlag.

Schmitt, C. (1969). *Gesetz und Urteil. Eine Untersuchung zum Problem der Rechtspraxis*. Verlag C.H. Beck.

Schmitt, C. (1950). *Ex Captivitate Salus. Erfahrungen der Zeit 1945/47*. Greven Verlag.

Schmitt, C. (1934). *Politische Theologie. Vier Kapitale zur Lehre von der Souveränität*. Verlag von Duncker & Humblot. Zweite Ausgabe.

Schmitt, C. (1932). *Der Begriff des Politischen*. Hanseatische Verlaganstalt.

Schmitt, C. (1923). "Soziologie des Souveränitätsbegriffes und politische Theologie". In *Hauptprobleme der Soziologie. Erinnerungsgabe für Max Weber*. Herausgegeben von Melchoir Palyi. *München und Leipzig: Verlag Von Duncker & Humblot, II*, 3–36.

Vaihinger, H. (1892). *Kommentar zu Kants Kritik der reinen Vernunft*. Union Deutsche Verlagsgesellschaft. Zweiter Band.

Vaihinger, H. (1881). *Kommentar zu Kants Kritik der reinen Vernunft*. Union Deutsche Verlagsgesellschaft. Erster Band.

Weber, M (2009). *Allgemeine Staatslehre und Politik (Staatssoziologie) Unvollendet. Mit- und Nachschriften 1920*. Herausgegeben von Gangolf Hübinger in Zusammenarbeit mit Andreas Terwey. Tübingen: J.C.B. Mohr (Paul Siebeck). *Max Weber Gesamtausgabe. III/7*.

Weber, M. (1994). *Wissenschaft als Beruf/Politik als Beruf*. Herausgegeben von Wolfgang J. Mommsen und Wolfgang Schluchter in Zusammenarbeit mit Birgitt Morgenbrod. Tübingen: J.C.B. Mohr (Paul Siebeck). *Max Weber Gesamtausgabe*. I/17.

CHAPTER 2

Schmitt, Bodin, and Hobbes on Sovereignty

Abstract In 1950 Schmitt published *Ex Captivitate Salus* in which he gave an account of the two times he was incarcerated by the Americans. Much of this book is depressing and not all that enlightening; however, there is one notable section that is highly revealing about how Schmitt viewed himself and his connection to law. In this section Schmitt maintained that the two "founders" of the modern theory of law, Jean Bodin and Thomas Hobbes, were basically like brothers to him. They shared the same need for order in the face of chaos; they both believed that law was based upon a sovereign. They all believed that the state needs a strong and decisive leader in order to survive. This chapter also included an examination of the doctrines of sovereignty that are found in the writings by Bodin and Hobbes and shows how much Schmitt relied on Bodin and Hobbes for his own theory of sovereignty in *Politische Theologie* and how much de departed from it.

Keywords Bodin · Hobbes · Sovereignty · "Recht" · Law

In 1950 Carl Schmitt published *Ex Captivitate Salus* and as the subtitle made clear, its contents referred to the years 1945, 1946, and 1947.

C. Adair-Toteff, *Schmitt on Sovereignty and the State of Exception*, Palgrave Studies in Classical Liberalism, https://doi.org/10.1007/978-3-031-91728-8_2

These three years were among the most difficult of Schmitt's often troubled life because it was during this time that he was twice incarcerated by the Americans. Reinhard Mehring sketched the last months of the Second World War and how Germany's defeat affected Schmitt's life. Mehring also described Schmitt's two arrests and his time spent in a cell. Schmitt was forbidden to write but Mehring indicated that much of *Ex Captivitate Salus* was written there. Mehring noted that an American allowed Schmitt to write and he used this time to document his thoughts (Mehring, 2009: 438–447). He was incarcerated beginning in September 1945 through October 1946 and again in February and March of 1947. He had lost his license to teach in September 1945 (Mehring, 1992: 129–189, 2009: 448–449). Mehring suggested that Schmitt and his second wife Duška often lived apart and that we know they corresponded regularly. However, there is not much available from these two years. We also know that Schmitt tended to view his circumstances from his own personal vantage point and that what he believed was not always reflective of the actual situation. This is particularly true regarding his collection *Ex Captivitate Salus*. Schmitt's "Gesprach mit Eduard Spranger" is an example of his ability to describe himself and events in the most favorable light; this life-long polemicist claimed that "I am a contemplative being" ("Ich bin ein kontemplative Mensch") and that he was never good at attacking and that he was defenseless. It was similar in tone to what he wrote in the beginning of "Historiographia in Nuce: Alexis de Tocqueville." There he wrote that what he had learned as a boy still rang true. "The victor writes the history." ("Der Sieger schreibt die Geschichte.") And to him that sounded, and sounds, like a command (Schmitt, 1950: 25). But he did write a number of things about himself that were absolutely true. He wrote that he was a jurist, a teacher, and a researcher. He also wrote with a fair degree of honesty and accuracy that he was a teacher and a researcher in the fields of "Völkerrecht" and "Verfassungsrecht." The latter is easily translated as "constitutional law" but the former is more difficult. "Recht" can mean "law" but in this case, it may also mean "right" or even a type of "justice." The main point is that it is not a strictly codified legal matter and that is because it does not apply to something specific and concrete as in a constitution, but involves something nebulous and almost spiritual as in the "Volk." "Völker" cannot just be translated as "peoples" and that is because "Volk" has moral and traditional connotations that are missing in the English "peoples." Perhaps the better rendering of "Volkerrecht" might be the "peoples' right" (Schmitt, 1950: 10–12, 55).

Schmitt began the chapter "Ex Captivitate Salus" with observation that during normal times, the jurist can be content to examine normal laws but that in times in which the threat of civil war is imminent, the jurist must be concerned with the prospects of war. Schmitt mentioned that there were types of wars that appeared in order and he considered the "holy war," the "just war," and the "duel war" as the types of wars that appear to be God approved if not God sanctioned. He connected this with the "Goddess of Justice" ("Göttin der Gerechtigkeit") (Schmitt, 1950: 58–59). Schmitt insisted that "My work is dedicated to the scholarly clarification of public law." ("Meine Arbeit ist der wissenschaftlichen Klärung des öffentlichen Rechts gewidment.") And he insisted that was not a positivistic legal system nor was it a "situationless generality" that applied in all worlds and in all time. Rather, it was a direct creation of Europe during the sixteenth and seventeenth centuries. This was the beginning of the age of "*jus publicum Europaeum*" and the beginning of the fame that "Teachers of Peoples' Right" ("Lehrer des Völkerrechts"). He noted that this included Fransisco de Vitoria, Albericus Gentilis, and Hugo Grotius. Schmitt insisted that he knows their work, their life, and the destiny as well as the history of their fame. He added that "I love them. They certainly belong to our camp." ("Ich liebe sie. Sie gehören durchaus zu unserem Camp.") But he immediately added that "They do not belong in my room." ("Sie gehören aber nicht in meiner Stube.") Instead, there are two who are closest to him and that he is daily in contact with them In addition, these two not only founded "Völkerrecht" but also founded "Staatsrecht." These two are Jean Bodin and Thomas Hobbes (Schmitt, 1950: 62–63). Schmitt explained that both Bodin and Hobbes come out of the age of the "confessional civil wars" ("konfessionallen Bürgerkriege"). Schmitt employed several ways to indicate his affinity with Bodin and Hobbes. He noted that they went from being names of living and present men to the names of brothers who he joined as a family member over the centuries. He also noted that beginning thirty years ago, "The invisible hand" ("Die unsichtbare Hand") not only led him again and again to Bodin's and Hobbes' books, but again and again to the most relevant pages. Schmitt insisted that their "manner of thinking and speaking" ("Denk- und Redeweise") have become those of a brother and that their answers to the questions of their days have become the answers to the questions of Schmitt's days (Schmitt, 1950: 64).

Bodin and Hobbes were both products of the religious civil wars but they were as dissimilar as two human beings could be. Bodin was a passionate legalist who was too often too passionate and was somewhat lacking in humor. He was as learned jurist as one from the school of Bartolus and he was as learned Humanist as one from the school of Cujaz, but unlike them, he always remained in his pragmatic profession. It was from that practical standpoint that he approached economic, philosophical, and theological questions (Schmitt, 1950: 65). This inclination toward pragmatism did not always serve Bodin well. Schmitt pointed out that Bodin often found himself in dangerous circumstances and toward the end of his life switched to the "wrong side" ("falsche Seite"). But Bodin remained neutral in the confessional conflicts and in general he promoted both tolerance and neutrality. Schmitt made his affinity to Bodin clear when he insisted that "Out of the pressure for public security and order developed the first judicially clear concept of European state law." ("Aus dem Drang nach öffentliche Sicherheit und Ordnung entstehen in seinem Kopf die ersten juristich klaren Begriffe des europäischen Staatsrechts.") (Schmitt, 1950: 65). The phrase "öffentiche Sicherheit und Ordnung" was taken from Artikel 48 of the Weimarer Reichsverfassung ("Weimar Reich Constitution") and was one of Schmitt's favorite phrases from the Weimar Era (1919–1933). Schmitt stressed "sovereignty" in Bodin's thinking by remarking that Bodin was the first to emphasize the sovereign state. He added that Bodin is one of those who helped with the birthing of the modern state ("Er ist einer der Gebursthelfer des modernen Staates.") What Bodin did not recognize in the "modern Leviathan" was that its form consists of "God and animal and man and machine" ("Gott und Tier und Mensch und Machine"). Bodin believed in "witches and demons" ("Hexen und Dämonen") and was critical of the Bible; but his "despair was not yet significant enough" ("Dafür war seine Verzweiflung noch nicht groß genug") (Schmitt, 1950: 65–66).

According to Schmitt, Thomas Hobbes was despairing enough and so he understood the modern Leviathan better than Bodin. Hobbes lived a century later and witnessed another round of theological conflicts and European civil wars, so "his despair is infinitely deeper than that of Bodin." ("seine Verzweiflung [ist] unendlich tiefer als die von Bodin.") It is probably revealing that Schmitt emphasized that Hobbes belonged to the greatest lonesome [people] of the seventeenth century. It is certainly revealing that Hobbes was attacked from all sides (Schmitt, 1950: 66).

Hobbes differed from Bodin in that he not only recognized the four-fold essence of the modern Leviathan but he also understood this critical importance of the individual. It was this emphasis on the individual that made Hobbes' thinking so dangerous. That and the fact that Hobbes rejected Bodin's political neutrality and embraced the clear line of demarcation of friendship. Hobbes differed from Bodin in that Hobbes was no practical man and no public person. Hobbes understood the need for protection and obedience and his fear and cautiousness allowed him to live to be ninety. As with Bodin, Hobbes was a Bible critic and fought against modern religion. "But while Bodin remained theologically pious and even superstitious, Hobbes is already an enlightener and an agnostic." ("Aber während Bodin theogisch fromm und sogar abergläubisch blieb, ist Hobbes bereits Aufklärer und Agnostiker.") (Schmitt, 1950: 67). Schmitt intoned that one should not talk about one's friends too much, but both Bodin and Hobbes were his friends. These friends differed greatly from each other yet were both products of their civil war eras (Schmitt, 1950: 67–68.) Bodin and Hobbes were founders of "public law" ("öffentliche Rechts") and both were superior figures and promoters of the separation of law from the Church (Schmitt, 1950: 72). Earlier Schmitt had noted that while the discipline of law had deep roots in Western Rationalism, its father was the reborn Roman law and its mother was the Roman Church. As "child" the "science of law" ("Rechtswissenschaft") clung to its father and left its mother's house. This separation took centuries and at the end of the old order the child found a new house and that house was the state. Schmitt emphasized the connection between public law and the sovereign state: "Still, the jurists of public law continued the doctrines and concepts of the sovereign state." (Doch führten den Juristen des öffentlicheen Rechts die Lehren und Begriffe vom souveränen Staate her weiter.") (Schmitt, 1950: 71). Schmitt made it clear his debt to Bodin and to Hobbes, but he did not discuss their doctrines of sovereignty.[1]

---

[1] Preston King was one of the scholars who published a comparison between Bodin and Hobbes. But his *Ideology of Order* is less an understanding of the two thinkers as it is a critique of absolutism. In addition, King ignored Schmitt's writings on Hobbes. King 1973.

BODIN AND HOBBES ON SOVEREIGNTY

The title of the English translation of Jean Bodin's *Six livres de la république* is somewhat misleading because it is *On Sovereignty*. However, the translator explained that his edition was limited to four chapters from Bodin's massive work and that these four contained Bodin's doctrine of sovereignty—the doctrine which made him famous. In his "Introduction" to his translation, Julian Franklin noted that it was Bodin's "precise definition of supreme authority" that helped him gain fame but also prompted criticism. Critics claimed that Bodin's notion of supreme authority was absolutist but Franklin argued that such criticism is unwarranted (Bodin, 1992: xii–xiii). Franklin had argued in his 1963 book that Bodin was not an absolutist but a universalist. He contended that Bodin's theory of law was superior to previous ones because it rested on principles which were derived from history and not from some absolutist first principle (Franklin, 1963: 67–70). In his 1973 book Franklin shifted his position and suggested that Bodin's theory did appear to embrace absolutism—if not in the *Six Books* then certainly in his later thinking (Franklin, 1973: 41–52). In neither of his two books nor in his translation of Bodin did Franklin mention either Hobbes or Schmitt. Yet Schmitt, and to a lesser extent Hobbes, was convinced that Bodin's authority was superior and that implies absolutism. How that claim stands up will be discussed in a later chapter; here it is important to discuss Bodin's doctrine of sovereignty.

Although Bodin is famous for his concept of sovereignty it does not appear until Chapter 8 in Book I of his great work. But it is clear from his definition that he regarded sovereignty as one of, if not the, most important concepts in ruling. He defined it as "Sovereignty is the absolute and perpetual power of a commonwealth."[2] This definition requires two points of clarification for Schmitt's understanding of sovereignty. First, that this power is "absolute" and that means that it cannot be limited by any one in any way. Second, this power is "perpetual" and while that would seem to be a given since the power is "absolute," Bodin wanted to ensure that it was not simply "absolute" for a specific time, but that it was

---

[2] Bodin (1992: 1). In his commentary on this definition Bernd Wimmer pointed out that the notion of "unlimited duration" ("unbegrentzen Dauer") was not just a major concern for Bodin but had been a concern for prior thinkers on ruling. Bodin (1981: 205, 590–591).

for all time. Bodin clarified that if someone is granted sovereign power for a specified time, then that individual cannot be regarded as a sovereign prince because that person is only a trustee. The person who confers that power can withdraw it; hence, it cannot be regarded as sovereign because it is not "absolute" (Bodin, 1992: 1–2). Bodin then provides a slightly enlarged definition: "Sovereignty, then, is not limited either in power, or in function, or in length of time" (Bodin, 1992). Bodin granted that there were individuals in history who abused their power but he maintained that they were not sovereigns, but were mere tyrants (Bodin, 1992: 4). Bodin admits that a person who clings to power after it has been withdrawn can still be regarded as a sovereign. That is because the person can be chosen by tacit consent or by force. But he is still a sovereign because he has power just as a robber has power. Note that neither the sovereign who remains in power by force nor the robber who takes money by force are considered "legal." Bodin explains this later by insisting that the prince is not subject to the law because "the very word 'law' in Latin implies the command of him who has the sovereignty" (Bodin, 1992: 6, 11). The notion of command is key: later Bodin writes "We thus see that the main point of sovereign majesty and absolute power consists of giving the law to subjects in general without their consent" (Bodin, 1992: 23, see 55). Consent implies agreement and agreement requires time. Bodin makes a point that will again be crucial for Schmitt. The captain of the ship needs to make a decision if he intends to avoid having the ship go down, so he cannot wait "on the opinion of the passengers" (Bodin, 1992: 24). Bodin emphasized in several places that the sovereign is above all human laws; the sovereign is subject only to God's laws and the laws of nature (Bodin, 1992: 13, 32, 36). In chapter 10 Bodin noted that the ability "to judge according to one's conscience" is a mark of every judge. But a sovereign is higher than a judge: "As for the title 'majesty,' it is clear that it belongs only to someone who is sovereign" (Bodin, 1992: 86–87). Bodin's concept of sovereignty was not the only thing that Schmitt appeared to share with Bodin; he also shared with him the notion of order. As W.H. Greenleaf argued, order "is the basis of all of Bodin's thought" (Greenleaf, 1973: 25).

"Order" was the basis of Hobbes' thinking as well. As Schmitt had pointed out in *Ex Captivitate Salus*, both Bodin and Hobbes wrote about sovereignty during times of civil war when there was little or no order.[3] While most commentators on Schmitt have overlooked Schmitt's connection to Bodin, a number of them have written on Hobbes' influence on him. Unfortunately, almost all neglected Bodin's theory of sovereignty and not many of them focused on Hobbes' conception of the sovereign.[4]

The philosophy of Thomas Hobbes is the subject of one of the most contentious disputes and has been since his own time (Bobbio, 1993: 69–70). Hobbes has been reviled as an atheist and as revolutionary. But he has also been indicted for his religious views and for being a reactionary. He is regarded as a philosopher of mechanics but also as a philosopher of individualism. Some critics have complained that Hobbes changed his mind within the same work. In effect, Hobbes has been attacked from all sides; a point that prompted Schmitt's appreciation. Among the most contentious of Hobbes' concepts is the concept of sovereignty. The account offered here is extremely brief and is not intended as a critical account. It is helpful to keep in mind that while Hobbes' most famous book is typically referred to as *Leviathan* it carried the subtitle *or The Matter, Forme, & Power of a Common-Wealth Ecclesiasticall and Civill* (Hobbes, 1992: 1). It is divided into four parts: "Of Man," "Of Common-Wealth," "Of A Christian Common-Wealth," and "Of The Kingdom of Darkness." Although Hobbes discussed theological sovereignty in the later parts, his notion of sovereignty is primarily found in the second part. But because his concept is dependent upon his notion of "Man" it is necessary to summarize a few points from the first part. Man is by nature a rational animal but he is moved by his passions. He is drawn to those things that are pleasurable and flees from those that cause fear. Pleasures and pains are not just physical; people relish honor and power and they avoid that which gives them shame and dishonor (Hobbes, 1992: 62–65). People are equal but in different ways; one person may have physical strength but another can counter that strength by cunning and reason. People may be sociable but they are prone to quarrel. Hobbes offers three causes: competition, diffidence, and glory.

---

[3] Toward the conclusion of "The Science in Hobbes's Politics" Tom Sorel noted that Carl Schmitt adapted Hobbes' theory to confront "German social disorders between the wars." Sorel (1989: 79).

[4] This is the case with almost all eleven of the essays found in the otherwise helpful collection on Hobbes and Schmitt. Part of this is because most of these scholars were considering Schmitt's later ideas about Hobbes in his later works.

The first is done for Gain, the second for Safety, and the third for Reputation. People quarrel over the most important things and the most trivial slights. This leads Hobbes to his famous contention that there is a "warre of every man against every man" and his famous dictum "the life of man [is] solitary, poore, nasty, brutish, and short" (Hobbes, 1992: 86–90). It is to avoid the natural state of war that people enter into contract (Hobbes, 1992: 96). The most important contract is that which forms the Common-Wealth (Hobbes, 1992: 117). One of the first points is that this is not a natural contract but is artificial. The second point is that people give up their rights in order to live. The third important point is that the person with the supreme authority is the sovereign (Hobbes, 1992: 120–121).

From the above Hobbes draws the following three conclusions: (1) that no one is obligated under any prior Covenant, (2) that the sovereign cannot breach the Covenant, and (3) by consenting to the sovereign, all must consent to his decrees (Hobbes, 1992: 122–123). Hobbes discusses the three forms of Common-Wealth: democracy, aristocracy, and monarchy, but he appears to prefer monarchy. Hobbes offers several reasons why he preferred the monarch—reasons which will be echoed by Schmitt. A king who has limited power cannot be a sovereign so he preferred a sovereign with full powers. The sovereign cannot forfeit or transfer his power (Hobbes, 1992: 134, 139). But Hobbes allowed that there are limits on the powers that the sovereign has: the sovereign cannot compel a subject to kill himself.[5] Later, in Chapter XXVI Hobbes repeats his claim that the sovereign is not bound by civil laws (Hobbes, 1992: 184). However, that does not mean that the sovereign is free to do whatever he wants. Both Bodin and Hobbes argued that the sovereign could not disobey the laws of nature and natural law (Bobbio, 1989: 12).

It was the noted Italian legal thinker Norberto Bobbio who was one of the few who recognized Hobbes' influence on Schmitt. Bobbio's interest in Hobbes manifested itself early with his review of Schmitt's 1938 book *Der Leviathan in der Staatslehre des Thomas Hobbes*. Bobbio concluded his review by indicating that Schmitt was correct in his claim that the symbol of the Leviathan obscured our understanding of Hobbes' theory but that

---

[5] Hobbes (1992: 151). The claim that a sovereign cannot order someone to kill himself is subject to debate. In fact, Hobbes' notion of justice is subject to debate. This debate is most interesting but is far beyond the scope of this book. Mention is made here only of D.D. Raphael's influential essay "Hobbes on Justice." Raphael (1989).

Schmitt acknowledged that Hobbes was "the most authentic master of a great political experience" (Bobbio, 1993: 212–214). But more recent discussions have cast further doubt on our understanding of the connection between Schmitt and Hobbes. Karsten Fischer maintained that "The nature of the relationship between Carl Schmitt and Thomas Hobbes has long vexed historians of political theory" (Fischer, 2011: 141). Fischer referred to another scholar who had claimed that Schmitt's assertion that he was a "brother" of Bodin and Hobbes was only "half-true" because Schmitt was attempting to deflect blame for his Nazi past away from himself. Regardless of Schmitt's political views of the 1930s, it is clear from his work on sovereignty that he was heavily indebted to Hobbes.

Concluding Comments

Because Carl Schmitt regarded himself in the long line of legal theorists going back to the sixteenth century and because he regarded himself as a "brother" to Bodin and Hobbes, it is crucial to have a basic understanding of the concepts of sovereignty which Bodin and Hobbes had promoted. Whether sovereignty is a necessary component of a commonwealth is not relevant here; what is, is that both Bodin and Hobbes emphasized the absolute power that the sovereign has and that the sovereign is necessary to maintain order and security. As Schmitt pointed out, Bodin and Hobbes lived during times of civil war and religious strife. During the 1920s there was not much religious strife in Germany, but Schmitt believed that Weimar was close to having a civil war. More importantly, Schmitt had a compelling need for "public security and order" ("öffentliche Sicherheit und Ordnung"). He would argue for that in many works, but especially in his work on sovereignty.

References

Bobbio, N. (1989). *Democracy and Dictatorship. The Nature and Limits of State Power* (P. Kennedy, Trans.). University of Minnesota Press.

Bobbio, N. (1993). *Thomas Hobbes and the Natural Law Tradition* (D. Gobetti, Trans.). University of Chicago Press.

Bodin, J. (1981). *Sechs Bücher über den Staat. Buch I-III*. Übersetzt und mit Anmerkungen von Bernd Wimmer. Eingeleitet und herausgegeben von P.C. Mayer-Tasch. Verlag C.H. Beck.

Bodin, J. (1992). *On Sovereignty. Four Chapters from The Six Books of the Commonwealth* (J. H. Franklin, Ed.). Cambridge University Press.

Fischer, K. (2011). Hobbes, Schmitt, and the Paradox of Religious Liberality. In J. Tralau (Ed.), *Thomas Hobbes and Carl Schmitt. The Politics of Order and Myth* (pp. 141–158). Routledge.

Franklin, J. (1963). *Jean Bodin and the Sixteenth-Century Revolution in the Methodology of Law and History.* Columbia University Press.

Franklin, J. (1973). *Jean Bodin and the Rise of Absolutist Theory.* Cambridge University Press.

Greenleaf, W. H. (1973). Bodin and the Idea of Order. In *Verhandlungen der internationalen Bodin Tagung in München.* Herausgegeben von Horst Denzer (pp. 23–38). Verlag C.H. Beck.

Hobbes, T. (1992). *Leviathan* (R. Tuck, Ed.). Cambridge University Press.

Hofmann, H. (2009). Auctoritas, non veritas, facit legem? In Stein, Buchstein, Offe (pp. 19–24).

King, P. (1974). *The Ideology of Order. A Comparative Analysis of Jean Bodin and Thomas Hobbes.* Barnes and Noble.

Mehring, R. (1992). *Carl Schmitt zur Einführung.* Junius.

Mehring, R. (2009). *Carl Schmitt. Aufstieg und Fall. Eine Biographie.* Verlag C.H. Beck.

Neumann, V. (2015). *Carl Schmitt als Jurist.* Mohr Siebeck.

Raphael, D. D. (1989). Hobbes on Justice. In G. A. J. Rogers & A. Ryan (Eds.), *Perspectives on Thomas Hobbes* (pp. 153–170). Clarendon Press.

Schmitt, C. (1950). *Ex Captvitate Salus. Erfahrungen der Zeit 1945/47.* Greven Verlag.

Sorel, T. (1989). The Science in Hobbes's Politics. In G. A. J. Rogers & A. Ryan (Eds.), *Perspectives on Thomas Hobbes* (pp. 67–80). Clarendon Press.

Stein, T., Buchstein, H., Offe, C. (Hg.) *Souveränität, Recht, Moral. Die Grundlagen politischer Gemeinschaft.* Campus Verlag.

CHAPTER 3

"Political Theology"?

Abstract There are many ideas in Schmitt's *Politische Theologie*. The book's title and subtitle indicate that the topics which he covers in this book include politics and theology as well as law, philosophy, and theology. The sheer breadth of Schmitt's learning is daunting enough. However, many scholars read his books as if they were normal works written by normal scholars. Schmitt's writings are not typical nor was Schmitt a typical author. He was always interested in the abnormal, the exceptional, and the unusual, and one understands his ideas better when one has a better understanding of Schmitt as a person. Schmitt's works are highly personal; what he experienced in life is often transferred into words. Schmitt also regarded life as a conflict and he frequently considered his critics to be enemies. This was certainly true regarding Hans Kelsen. It is Kelsen who is frequently attacked in Schmitt's works, but there are others as well in *Politische Theologie*. Schmitt often accused others of not providing answers and being too polemical. *Politische Theologie* is a polemical work and while it is ostensibly about "political theology" he does not really provide a definition of what that is.

Keywords Political theology · Law · Sociology · Kelsen

© The Author(s), under exclusive license to Springer Nature   23
Switzerland AG 2025
C. Adair-Toteff, *Schmitt on Sovereignty and the State of Exception*,
Palgrave Studies in Classical Liberalism,
https://doi.org/10.1007/978-3-031-91728-8_3

There are many ideas encapsulated in Carl Schmitt's *Politische Theology*. As the title and subtitle indicate, Schmitt's work encompasses politics and theology, as well as law, philosophy, and sociology. The breadth of Schmitt's scholarly interests is daunting and whereas many scholars can be read without knowing much about the biographic details of the author, that cannot be said regarding Carl Schmitt. As Reinhard Mehring has pointed out in several of his books on Schmitt, much of Schmitt's scholarship was infused with personal factors. Mehring maintained that Schmitt was one of the few professors who used his pen to draw blood and employed concepts as weapons of war (Mehring, 1992: 7, 2014: V). Schmitt regarded his scholarly critics as enemies and he was convinced that many were arrayed against him. The scholar whom Schmitt regarded as his greatest enemy was the legal theorist and constitutional scholar Hans Kelsen. Kelsen was an Austrian but he moved to Germany in the 1920s. It is on good grounds that Kelsen experts and Schmitt scholars have agreed that Kelsen and Schmitt were "antipodes" (Dreier, 2021: 10, 90; Mehring, 2014: 50, 53, 84; Métall, 1969: 1, 61; Noack, 1993: 32; Schuett, 2021: 4). Although Schmitt and Kelsen were adversaries, both were polarizing. For much of the 1920s, Schmitt's opposition to Kelsen was based upon their differences regarding parliament, democracy, and law. Part of Schmitt's complaint about Kelsen was his religious background, but that did not surface until the 1930s. However, Schmitt's biographers have suggested that *Politische Theologie* should be read as a theological treatise because of Schmitt's Catholicism. Noack and Mehring pointed to Schmitt's booklet from 1924—*Römischer Katholizismus und politische Form*. Because Noack and Mehring believed that that book was a key writing, they tended to view *Politische Theologie* as an earlier religious text. Hence, they have overlooked the dominate topic of sovereignty. Yet, both also acknowledged Schmitt's fractious relationship with the Roman Catholic Church; a relationship that was fractious because of the breakup of Schmitt's first marriage (Mehring, 1992: 53–54; Noack, 1993: 64–65). There is little doubt that religion in general and Catholicism in particular often played a role in Schmitt's thinking, but there should also be little doubt that the book that is the most closely related to *Politische Theology* is *Die Diktatur*. This is evident from three things. First, it carries the subtitle *Von Anfängen des modernen Souveränitätsgedanken bis zum proletarischen Klassenkampf.* Second, Schmitt made it clear that his thesis was bound up with the notion of the "state of exception" ("Ausnahmezustand") which directly connects *Die Diktatur* to *Politische*

Theologie (Schmitt, 1921: VI). Third, to make the connection between the notion of "Ausnahmezustand" in both the 1921 book and the 1922 book, Schmitt added an appendix: "Die Diktatur des Reichspräsidenten nach Art. 48 der Weimarer Verfassung." Schmitt added this appendix to the 1928 edition of *Die Diktatur* because Art. 48 of the Weimarer Reichsverfassung focused on the powers that the Reichspräsident was given to restore "public security and order" ("öffentliche Sicherheit und Ordnung") (Schmitt, 1928: 213–259). It may be significant that most of Schmitt's writings have been published by Duncker & Humblot but *Römischer Katholizismus und politischer Form* was not.[1]

Although the opening sentence in *Politische Theologie* may seem straightforward, it is more complex than it seems. That is because it contains terms that had a particular context when Schmitt published it in the early 1920s. "Souverän ist, wer über den Ausnahmezustand entscheidet." Again, this is a possible translation: "Sovereign is the one who decides about the state of exception" (Schmitt, 1922: 11, 1923: 5). Although Schmitt designates this as his definition, all of the first chapter is spent clarifying it. What he did not clarify was the term "Ausnahmezustand." It is the "state of exception" and while it is often treated as a "state of emergency," Schmitt's emphasis is not on "emergency" but on "exception." This is an important point to keep in mind because much of Schmitt's thinking lies beyond legality. Much of Chapter II is used by Schmitt to contrast his politics of exception with Hans Kelsen's normal legality.

Carl Schmitt insisted that the concept of sovereignty was not a normal concept but was what he referred to as a "Grenzbegriff." This "limit concept" or "borderline concept" is not to be considered a "confused concept" as it is used in the "unclean terminology [of the] popular literature" ("unsaubern Terminologie popular Literatur"). Instead, it is a concept of the "furthermost sphere" ("äußeresten Sphäre"). Schmitt clarifies what he means by "Grenz" when he contrasts his definition of sovereignty with one that is far removed from "Normalfall" ("normal case") but is connected to the "Grenzfall" ("borderline case"). This is the "Ausnahmezustand" ("state of exception") and this state differs from

---

[1] It was published by J.G. Cotta' sche Buchhandlung Nachfolger. One of the most similar ideas from *Römischer Katholizismus und politische Form* to *Politische Theologie* was Schmitt's opposition between "Diktatur und Anarchie." Schmitt (2016: 28).

both a "Notverordnung" ("Emergency order") or a "Belagerungszu-stand" ("state of occupation"). The "Ausnahmezustand" is a general concept in "Staatslehre" ("theory of the state") and is particularly suited for a juridical definition of sovereignty. It is particularly suited because it has a "systematischen, rechtslogischen Grund" ("systematic, legal-logical foundation"). Although Schmitt does not mention this, he implicitly distinguishes between decisions made in normal cases and decisions made in unusual and abnormal cases: "Die Entscheidung über die Ausnahme ist nämlich im eminenten Sinne Entscheidung." ("The decision regarding the exception is certainly in the most eminent sense [the] decision." This is because a regular norm such as a normal legal principle cannot apply because it lies outside the purview of normal law. He suggests that the legal theorist and Tübingen professor of law Robert Mohl (1899–1875) was confused when he suggested that the test whether there is a "Not-stand" ("state of emergency") exists is how the legal system addresses it. But Schmitt counters that that is exactly what needs to be determined and he suggests that Mohl took the position that he did because he was a member of the older "Legal State Liberalism." As a result, he regarded decisions as normal legal questions and did not comprehend that decisions regarding the "state of exception" are not normal but are exceptional (Schmitt, 1923: 5, 1934: 11, 2015: 13).

Schmitt indicated his dissatisfaction with the abstractness of a typical definition of sovereignty as the highest power because it lacked conceptual rigor. One may dispute the practical or theoretical aspects of the concept of sovereignty but one has to concede that it applies to the dangerous situations of conflicts, regardless whether one calls them conflicts of state interest, conflicts regarding "public security and order" ("öffentliche Sicherheit und Ordnung"). It did not seem to matter to Schmitt what governments called such conflicts; what mattered was that they were abnormal situations which then required abnormal means to deal with them. What this means is that this requires someone who is astute enough and knowledgeable enough to recognize such a "state of excep-tion." But here the normal legal authority lacks the knowledge and the ability to recognize that this "state" is "exceptional." Thus, it lies outside the normal legal authority's sphere of competency. Perhaps Schmitt was thinking specifically about the Weimar Constitution because he noted that the most a constitution can do is to recognize who is capable of dealing with such a "state of exception." In Schmitt's view, the need for balance and harmony in a constitution makes it unsuitable to make decisive decisions that a "state of exception" demands. In effect, the constitution is unable to determine who is the sovereign. Again, Schmitt emphasizes that the constitution covers normal cases and is unsuited to deal with exceptions. In fact, most modern constitutions do not even deal with the notion of sovereignty. They do not even want to address the possibility that a constitution can be suspended. He adds that all of the developments of the modern legal state theories of Hans Kelsen and Hugo Krabbe and that Schmitt will address some of those issues in his subsequent chapter. For now, Schmitt insists that the question of whether an "extreme case of exception" ("extreme Ausnahmefall") can be banished from the world is itself not a legal question. Instead, whether it is possible is solely dependent upon one's philosophical convictions; specifically upon one's philosophy of history or one's metaphysical convictions (Schmitt, 1934: 6, 13, 2015: 14).

Schmitt then turns his attention to the history of the concept of sovereignty. He complains that there have been a few who have touched upon this history but most have not taken the trouble of trying to understand the concept and its history. Specifically, Schmitt complains that few go beyond the abstract formulations in textbooks and only regard sovereignty as the "highest power" ("höchsten Macht"). But this is nothing more than "the endless repetition of the totally empty manner of speaking of the highest power" ("die endlos wiederholt, völlig leere Redensart von der höchsten Macht"). Schmitt further complains that no one has closely investigated what the famous authors of the concept of sovereignty meant by that. It is Bodin who first developed a concise notion of sovereignty. Schmitt notes that people refer to Bodin's often cited claim that "sovereignty is the absolute and perpetual power in a republic" (la souveraineté est la puissance absolue et perpétuelle d'une République"). But he insists that Bodin was far better in setting out what sovereignty meant in Chapter Ten of Book One. It is there that Bodin offered "the beginning of the modern doctrine of state" ("der Anfang der modernen Staatslehre"). There Bodin provided a number of practical comments but each of them led back to the question: "How much is the sovereign bound to the laws and obligated to the nobles?" Schmitt suggests that this question is extremely important because Bodin maintained that one is obligated to fulfill promises because that is based upon natural law. However, Bodin also maintained that in a "case of emergency" ("Notfall"), the obligations which are based upon natural law cease to apply. Schmitt argued that Bodin's sense of obligation rested on the promise to fulfill that which is in the interest of the people but when that which is necessary and urgent arises, then the obligation ceases. Schmitt also notes that that notion was nothing new. What was new was Bodin's contention that this was "a simple either-or" ("ein einfaches Entweder-Oder") relationship and that the "Notfall" reveals this. It was to Bodin's credit that he regarded the sovereign as the "indivisible unity" ("unteilbare Einheit") and that he was the one who decided the answer regarding the power of the state. To quote Schmitt: "His scholarly achievement and the reason for his success therefore lies in that he introduced the decision into the concept of the sovereignty." ("Seine wissenschaftliche Leistung und der Grund seines Erfolges liegen also darin, daß er die Dezision in den Souveränitätsbegriff hineingetragen hat.") (Schmitt, 1923, 1934: 14, 2015: 15).

In the 1922 book, its reproduction in the 1934 edition, and the 1923 version, there is no break. But in the tenth edition of *Politische Theologie*, the sentence which follows the one just given begins a new paragraph. Schmitt repeats his earlier complaint that people simply recite Bodin's comment that the sovereign is the highest power. But Schmitt expands on his earlier criticism by pointing out that virtually no one focuses on the key aspect which lies behind this definition. Before continuing, it is helpful to return to what Bodin actually wrote in Chapter 10. There he insisted that the main purpose of that chapter is to identify the marks of the sovereign. Unfortunately, most of those thinkers who preceded Bodin did not think it important to do so. Bodin turned to Aristotle who also did not discuss the sovereign, but he did differentiate among the three parts of the state. Bodin added that we should regard these three parts as the three aspects of the sovereign. These are (1) to deliberate and take counsel, (2) to create officers and to establish their duties, and (3) to render justice. But Bodin insisted that it is a counsel that should deliberate; it is a counsel that should appoint the officers and determine their duties, and all princes dispense justice. Therefore, none of Aristotle's marks apply to the sovereign. Therefore, the true mark of the sovereign must be found elsewhere (Bodin, 1992: 47, 50). Bodin then maintained that the first mark of the sovereign is to give laws. But Bodin added that the sovereign determines his laws without needing the consent of anyone (Bodin, 1992: 56, 59). Much of Chapter 10 is filled with historical examples from antiquity as well as from Bodin's own era. Many of his comments go beyond laws such as his extensive discussion about taxation. Therefore, it is hard to find any specific passage that Schmitt insists is the main question for Bodin. This question is whether the sovereign gives up his sovereignty if he follows through with his promises to either the nobles or to the people ("Volk). According to Schmitt, the sovereign is entitled to break his promise or to alter the laws or to rescind the laws in their entirety when there is the (emergency) need to do so (Schmitt, 1923: 7, 1934: 14, 2015: 15). Schmitt is correct to point to Bodin's reluctance to allow either the nobles or the counsel any say in such matters because that would make the sovereign's decision dependent on others. In Schmitt's opinion, this would be an absurdity in Bodin's account—an absurdity that Bodin himself ruled out. He could not envision a sovereign who would need to give the people or the nobles the right to be "ruler" ("Herr"). Schmitt concludes that in the general case as well as the particular case, only the sovereign has the right and the power to set aside laws. Schmitt insisted that it was the mark of Bodin's sovereign that only he was able to "declare war and conclude peace, appoint the officials, make final determinations, have the right to pardon, etc." ("Kriegerklärung und Friedensschluß, Ernennung der Beamten, letzte Instanz, Begnadigungsrecht usw.") (Schmitt, 1923: 7, 1934: 15, 2015: 16).

Schmitt refers to his book *Die Diktatur* where he claimed to have shown that the main function of the dictator is to make decisions regarding the "state of exception" ("Ausnahmezustand"). He further claimed that he had shown how historically this decision-making was the mark of the sovereign. This was true, he claimed, in respect to the natural law theorists of the seventeenth century. In fact, Schmitt insisted that the question regarding the sovereign was nothing other than the question regarding who was entitled to make the decision about the "state of exception." This was particularly true regarding the work of Pufendorf. Yet, examining *Die Diktatur* Pufendorf is mentioned only in passing in Schmitt's discussion about Hobbes.[2] Since Schmitt introduces his earlier ideas into the exploration of sovereignty, it is legitimate to detour briefly and to consider what he wrote about Bodin and Hobbes in *Die Diktatur.*

---

[2] Schmitt (1928: 24, 32). The 1928 edition of *Die Diktatur* is an unchanged version of the 1921 edition. As with *Politische Theologie* Schmitt added a new foreword. As with the 1934 edition of *Politische Theologie,* the 1928 edition of *Die Diktatur* is (relatively) easier to obtain.

Schmitt regarded Bodin as a forerunner to his own concept of a dictator. He insisted that Bodin recognized that the issue of a dictatorship is not a juridical problem but a political one. That is because the dictator is concerned with power and not with justice. But Schmitt was interested in utilizing Bodin's concept of the sovereign for his own use. That is why Schmitt insisted that "Bodin did not differentiate between the sovereignty of the state and the possessor of state power." ("Bodin unterscheidet nicht zwischen der Souveränität des Staates und der des Trägers der Staatsgewalt.") It is also why Schmitt wrote: "He saw no essential difference between dictatorship and sovereignty." ("Er sieht keinen wesentlichen Unterschied zwischen Diktatur und Souveränität.") (Schmitt, 1928: 27–29). But Schmitt's purpose was to use Bodin's concept of the sovereign for his own notion of a legitimate dictatorship. This was to argue that the modern conception of sovereign dictatorship was fundamentally at odds with the dictatorship of the proletariat. How successful he was in that argument is beyond these concerns here.

To return to the first chapter of *Politische Theologie*, Schmitt insisted that the question regarding the sovereign is connected to the issue of not just "bellum omnium contra omnes" but is bound up with the issue of the disruption of "public security and order" ("öffentliche Sicherheit und Ordnung") so that it is crucial to determine what that means and what the disturbance entails. He suggested that it means one thing to the "military bureaucracy" ("miltarische Bureaukratie") and another to the "businessman-like spirit" ("kaufmännische Geist"). Schmitt argues that despite this difference, the determination of "public security and order" is a decision, just as any question regarding when that "public security and order" is under threat of disturbance or actual disruption is also a decision. He concludes that paragraph with the observation "Also the legal order, as every order, rests on a decision and not on a norm." ("Auch die Rechtsordnung, wie jede Ordnung, beruht auf einer Entscheidung und nicht auf einer Norm.") (Schmitt, 1923: 7, 1934: 16, 2015: 16).

Schmitt turns to the question whether there can be earthly sovereigns or whether only God is the sole sovereign. Schmitt notes that this was a much-disputed question during the seventeenth century, if not before. It was questionable whether a king or the lord of an estate or the "Volk" could be regarded as sovereign. He regards this as the issue of the subject of sovereignty, or as he also states, the application of a concept to concrete instances. Once again, Schmitt returns to Bodin's account of sovereignty. As already suggested, Bodin maintained that there are such entities as earthly sovereigns and he had provided several of the markings or characteristics of worldly sovereigns. One of Schmitt's points is that Bodin's successors relied on his account to determine what "authority" or "power" the sovereign possessed.[3] If Bodin's French successors had no difficulties in appropriating his account, the Germans had numerous problems. Schmitt again complained about the lack of conceptual clarity and he noted that some German legal scholars did not doubt these characteristics and drew conclusions from that while others had considerable doubts regarding the same characteristics and drew opposing conclusions. These conflicting conclusions were regarded as necessary, which led to an even more intensive controversy. Schmitt suggested that the controversy really revolved around the question of who had authority for occurrences for which there were no predictions. In other words, for those instances that were exceptional and unforeseeable. This was a case for "not limited power" ("nicht begrenzten Macht"). He continued that this was the discussion of the "case of exception" ("Ausnahmefall")— the "extremus necessitates casus." This is not merely an "exceptional case"; rather, it is the most extreme state of emergency. Schmitt suggests that the issue regarding the monarchy is reflected in the "legal-logical structure" ("rechtslogischen Struktur"). Schmitt once again notes that the scholars who discuss this notion tend to regard everything from the point of normalcy. In so doing, they ignore the fact that the "exceptional case" is exactly that—exceptional. Instead, they consider and they judge everything in accordance to the relevant constitutional points. Thus, they ignore the fact that constitutions are written according to norms and for normal cases. He suggests that in effect they have been "asking" constitutions about questions that constitutions cannot "answer." Schmitt pointed particularly to a controversy from the previous century where legal scholars had a debate. The issue was, under the German constitution of 1871, whether member states were actually sovereign states or were they merely members of the newly unified Germany. Unfortunately, both sides of this debate regarded this as a legal and a constitutional

---

[3] It is noteworthy that the term "Befugnis" can be translated as "authority" and "power." What is just as noteworthy is that the Brothers Grimm devote only one very small paragraph to "Befugnis" in their thirty-three-volume dictionary. They cite Kant, Schelling, and Goethe but point out that Kant considered this a part of morality, Schelling considered it a matter of class and standing, whereas Goethe thought it to be a neutral term. Grimm (1854: 1274).

matter, not recognizing that it was a political matter with political rami-fications. This is something that legal scholars have tended to do but often with inappropriate results. Schmitt's criticism was trained on the "proof" that the sides used. That is, they attempted to decide whether an individual German state was sovereign or not based upon whether the state's legal standing was determined by the "concept of derivability or non-derivability" ("Begriff der Ableitbarkeit oder Nicht-Arbleitbarkeit." In Schmitt's opinion, what was far more relevant was the question about the standing of the states as determined by constitution; that is, the federal government had no limits whereas the state governments did.

The constitution from 1919 was far better suited to address this same issue. The Weimarer Reichsverfassung from August 1919 included Art. 48. In 1922, this article was subject to discussion and open to debate, but it had not begun to draw attention and generate controversy as it would later during the Weimar Era. Art. 48 was specifically written to address the "state of exception" ("Ausnahmezustand").[4] Composed of five para-graphs, the first two gave the Reichspräsident the authority to intervene in the internal affairs of a German state ("Land") if (a) they fail to fulfill their obligations and (b) if they fail to restore "public security and order" ("öfftentliche Sicherheit und Ordnung"). The Reichspräsident was autho-rized to intervene and use any force he deemed necessary including the use of weapons (Preuß, 2015: 605–606). Schmitt emphasizes the unlim-ited power that the Reichspräsident was given under Art. 48 with the only genuine check being Parliament. However, it was limited to the issue of the duration of the "state of exception." He further explains that this was not the question regarding sovereignty as it was of the ques-tion of possible conceptual limits. He clarifies that in his opinion, this only affected the form and not the content and that Art. 48 gave the Reichspräsident an unlimited power. Schmitt likened that to the Art. 14 of the Charte from 1815 which made the monarch into the sovereign. He maintained that if according to Art. 48 the individual states do not have the power "to declare a state of exception" ("Ausnahmezustand zu erklären"), then they are not states. Schmitt summarizes this by insisting "The specific focus of the question of whether the German "states" are

---

[4] For an account of Art. 48, its meaning, its history, and its function during the Weimar Era, see *Dictatorial Power and the State of Exception. The Controversial Article 48 in the Weimar Constitution. 1919–1933.* Adair-Toteff (2025).

states or not lies in Art. 48." ("In Artikel 48 liegt der eigentliche Schwerpunkt der Frage, ob die deutschen Länder Staaten sind oder nicht." (Schmitt, 1923: 8, 1934: 18, 2015: 18).

It is a matter of sovereignty if there is an attempt to limit the power to address the "state of exception" in respect to its duration. It is also a matter of sovereignty if there is an attempt to limit the number of steps that the sovereign can take to address a "state of exception." In fact, these attempts are steps backward and must be addressed. But here, Schmitt maintains that jurisprudence is oriented to "the questions of daily life and the ongoing businesses" ("den Fragen des täglichen Lebens und der laufenden Geschäfte") and has "no interest in the concept of sovereignty" ("kein Interesse an dem Begriff der Souveränität"). Jurisprudence regards only the normal as understandable and anything else is a disruption. Jurisprudence can only stand bewildered facing "the extreme case" ("den extremen Fall"). But not every demand for extraordinary authority is a "state of exception" ("Ausnahmezustand")—a state of police emergency is not an "Ausnahmezustand" nor is it a state of emergency. The "Ausnahmezustand" belongs to an unlimited authority. That means the suspension of the entire normal order. As he insists "It is clear that when this condition arises, the state remains while justice retreats." ("Ist dieser Zustand eingetreten, so ist klar, daß der Staat bestehen bleibt, während das Recht zurücktritt.") For Schmitt, the state is what is all important; all else is subservient to the state. This is the case with respect to the validity of any legal order. "The decision makes itself independent of any normative binding and in this specific sense becomes absolute." ("Die Entscheidung mach sich frei von jeder normativen Gebundenheit und wird im eigentlichen Sinne absolut.") (Schmitt, 1923: 9, 1934: 19, 2015: 18). To make this clearer, Schmitt insists that in the "case of exception" ("Ausnahmefall") the state suspends the "law" ("Recht") and creates its own law. This is because Schmitt believes that the concept "law-order" ("Rechts-Ordnung") contains two elements: one is the norm and the other is the decision. In normal cases, there is no opposition or even conflict between the two elements. In normal times, the two elements are part of the juridical system. However, in the "case of exception" ("Ausnahmefall") the decision comes to the front while the norm is negated.

Thus far, Schmitt has not mentioned sociology but now he brings it up. Partially this is because the Palyi collection is sociologically oriented and partially because it honored Max Weber. Schmitt addresses the sociological part in this chapter but will briefly discuss Weber in the following chapters. Schmitt's main point is that the need for a decision in the "case of exception" ("Ausnahmefall") is not a sociological matter. He arrives at that point by indicating that this is not an either-or disjunction and that just because the "Ausnahmefall" lacks a juridical significance does not make it a part of "sociology" (Schmitt's quotation marks). Schmitt insists that the "Ausnahmefall" is not something that is subsumable but is distinct from the general [legal] conception. As a result, the decision is "in absolute purity" ("in absoluter Reinheit"). Schmitt again insists that a general norm is connected with daily living and as such, normal rules dominate. But "The norm needs a homogeneous medium." ("Die Norm braucht ein homogenes Medium.") (Schmitt, 1923: 9, 1934: 19, 2015: 19). He insists that the factual normativity is not some "external presupposition" ("äußere Voraussetzung") (Schmitt's quotation marks) which can be simply ignored. Rather it is an essential part of justice. In a remarkable sentence Schmitt declares "There is no norm that would be applicable to chaos." ("Es gibt keine Norm, die auf ein Chaos anwendbar wäre.") Schmitt repeats his insistence that laws and norms have validity only during normal times and under normal conditions. An order must be developed only in situations where an order makes sense. But it is the sovereign who determines whether the situation is a normal one or whether it is an abnormal one. If it is normal, then normal directives are acceptable; but if the situation is abnormal, then normal directives not only do not apply, but there is no possible justification for even asking whether they apply (Schmitt, 1923: 9, 1934: 20, 2015: 19).

The 2015 edition has a new paragraph where the essay of 1923 and the second edition of the book from 1934 did not. This break appears to be needed because Schmitt's tone has shifted and his claims have become stronger. This is true regarding the final two and a half pages of this chapter. This shift in tone is evident in the first several sentences: "All law is 'situational law.'" ("Alles Rechts ist 'Situationsrecht.'") It is not exactly clear what he means by "situational law"—does it mean that the situation determines the law or that law governs the situation? The following sentence does not do much to answer that question: "The sovereign creates and guarantees the situation as a whole in its entirety." ("Der Souverän schaff und garantiert die Situation als Ganzes in ihrer Totalität.") But the third sentence clarifies Schmitt's point: "He has the monopoly for this final decision." ("Er hat das Monopol dieser letzten Entscheidung.") Schmitt emphasizes this point by declaring that this monopoly is the essence of the sovereign. The sovereign's essence lies in his ability to make decisions, not in the power to force or the power to dominate. This sentence is a clear break with Max Weber. Again, one needs to keep in mind that the 1923 version was in the second volume of the work dedicated to the memory of Max Weber. And, that Schmitt had participated in Weber's final seminar on the sociology of the state (Weber, 2009: 50). In "Politik als Beruf" Weber had defined the state not according to what it is but what it does. What a state does is exert force or merely threaten to exert force. Weber believed that power and force ("Macht" and "Gewalt") were the defining characteristics of the state. He quoted Trotsky's claim "Every state is founded on force." ("Jeder Staat wird auf Gewalt gegründet.") And he added "That in fact is correct." Weber continued that the mark of the state is that it has the monopoly on the legitimate force (Weber, 1994: 157–158). Weber gave the lecture "Politik als Beruf" on January 28, 1919. In his "Staatssoziologie" from the Spring Semester of 1920, Weber repeated his claim that the state has the monopoly on physical force (Weber, 2009: 74–77). Schmitt continued to agree with Weber's claim that the definition of a state is not what it is, but what it does. But Schmitt preferred to think of this as the "essence" ("Wesen") of the state, rather than an indication ("Merkmal") of the state. Far more importantly, Schmitt rejected Weber's claim that domination and force are the primary features of the state. Instead, the essential feature of a state was the sovereign who has the power to make decisions. The sovereign decides in all cases; normal cases require normal decisions, but the "Ausnahmefall" demands a specific and abnormal decision. Schmitt claims: "The case of exception reveals the essence of the stately authority the clearest." ("Der Ausnahmefall offenbart das Wesen der staatlichen Autorität am klarsten.")[5] Schmitt differentiates the decision from the "legal norm" ("Rechtsnorm") and he grants that it may seem paradoxical to say that this proves that the authority creates the law, rather than needing to have the law (Schmitt, 1923: 10, 1934: 20, 2015: 19).

Schmitt abruptly returns to previous thinkers and he points out that for John Locke and other rationalist thinkers of the eighteenth

---

[5] Another difference between Schmitt and Weber is that the former uses the word "authority" ("Autorität") whereas Weber used the term "Herrschaft" which can be translated as "domination," "rule," as well as "authority." Weber also insists that the ruler has the power to compel people to obey; Schmitt is uninterested in the subjects; his concern is only with the sovereign.

century, the "case of exception" ("Ausnahmefall") is something to be ignored. Schmitt maintained that the relatively orderly eighteenth century prompted those thinkers to forget the importance of the "Ausnahmefall" for the disorder of the previous century. He adds that "For Kant, the emergency law is no longer a law." ("Für Kant, ist das Notrecht überhaupt kein Recht mehr.") For his contemporaries, there are two divergent approaches. For the Neo-Kantians, such as Kelsen, it is self-evident that they ignore the "case of exception." Kelsen's legal philosophy will become more prominent in the next chapter. Here, Schmitt is more concerned with the legal rationalists as a whole and not just with the Neo-Kantians. Schmitt's criticism rests on two grounds.

One, the rationalists are always preoccupied with the normal cases because they insist these cases are subject to calculability and, as a result, to predictability. Schmitt contends that such claims of predictability are misguided and even the notion of calculability is wrong. It is a mistake to think that law is rational and therefore deals only with the normal cases. However, even the rationalists need to admit that exceptional cases do exist. The rationalists are unable to deal with these because they lie outside of the zone of the norm. In fact, the rationalists are unable to confront the "case of exception" because it does not, and cannot, fit within the rationalists' judicial framework. Schmitt insists that the "Ausnahmefall" is problematic because it is the case in which the law is suspended. He clarifies this by pointing to the suggestion that the exceptional case proves nothing and only the normal cases prove anything. What the exceptional case does do is upset the "unity and order of the rationalistic schema" ("Einheit und Ordnung des rationalistischen Schemas"). But Schmitt also mentions that it is not just the rationalists who think this but that legal positivists such as Gerhard Anschütz do as well. It is a fact that the "Ausnahmefall" is not a matter for law but actually is outside of the law. That is why Anschütz admits that "The state law stops here." ("Das Staatsrecht hört hier auf.") (Schmitt, 1923: 10, 1928: 8, 20–21, 2015: 9, 20–21). This leads to Schmitt's second point.

Two, rather than being uninteresting, it is actually the exceptional case that generates interest. Schmitt explains that "concrete life" does not step back from the "Ausnahmefall" but must confront it as it contains that which is most interesting. He insists that the claim "the exception is more interesting than the rule" is not "a Romantical irony for the paradox" ("einer romantischen Ironie für das Paradoxe"). Instead, it contains that which provides insight. This provides a clearer insight than the generalization of the average gained from the repetitive. As Schmitt insists: "The case of the exception is more interesting that the normal case." ("Der Ausnahmefall ist interessaner als der Normalfall.") He immediately adds "The normal proves nothing, the exception proves all." ("Das Normale beweist nichts, die Ausnahme beweist alles.") The "Ausnahmefall" provides "actual life" with the power to break through the "crust formed by a repetition of a frozen mechanism." ("Kruste einer in Wiederholung erstarrten Mechanik.")

Schmitt concludes Chapter I with a quotation from an unidentified Protestant theologian. This quotation is important for at least three reasons. First, it is the lengthiest quotation of the entire book. Second, it comes at the very end of the chapter. Third, and most importantly, Schmitt evidently believed that it forcefully made his case for why and how the exceptional case is more instructive; hence, more valuable, than the normal case. These are three valid reasons for investigating this quotation.

In terms of length, the quotation takes up ten lines or a third of a page. In terms of placement, it comes at the very end of Chapter one. Schmitt concludes the chapter with this quotation. He does not add any comment; he apparently believed that the quotation spoke of itself. In terms of importance, Schmitt was evidently convinced that the quotation made his case that that which is typical is uninteresting, if not irrelevant. Only that which is an exception is interesting and relevant. Perhaps more importantly, only the exceptional case can teach us anything of value.

This is a translation of the passage that Schmitt provides:

> The exception explains the general and itself. And if one wants to correctly study the general, then one needs only to turn one's attention to an actual exception. It [the exception] is much more clearly reflected to the day than the general. In the long run, the eternal talk about the general will be tedious; there are exceptions. If one cannot explain them, then one cannot also explain the general. Normally, one does not notice the difficulty because one does not think of the general with passion; but rather, thinks of it with a comfortable superficiality. In contrast to the general, one thinks about the exception with aggressive passion. (Schmitt, 1923: 11, 1934: 22, 2015: 21)

This is the passage that Schmitt gives:

Die Ausnahme erklärt das Allgemeine und sich selbst. Und wenn man das Allgemeine richtig studieren will, braucht man sich nur nach einer wirklichen Ausnahme umzusehen. Sie legt alles viel deutlicher an den Tag als das Allgemeine selbst. Auf die Länge wird man des ewigen Geredes vom Allgemeinen überdrüssig; es gibt Ausnahmen. Kann man sie nicht erklären, so kann man auch das Allgemeine nicht erklären. Gewöhnlich merkt man die Schwierigkeit nicht, weil man nicht einmal mit Leidenschaft, sondern mit einer bequemen Oberflächlichkeit denkt. Die Ausnahme dagegen denkt das Allgemeine mit energischer Leidenschaft.

Here is Kierkegaard's original:

Die Ausnahme erklärt also das Allgemeine und sich selbst, und wenn man das Allgemeine recht studieren will, braucht man sich nur nach einer wirklichen Ausnahme umzusehen. Sie legt alles viel deutlicher an den Tag als das Allgemeine selbst....
Auf die Länge wird man des ewigen Geredes vom Allgemeinen und Allgemeinen überdrüssig, das man so oft wiederholt, bis es langweilig wird. Es gibt Ausnahmen, Kann man sie nicht erklären, so kann man auch das Allgemeine nicht erklären. Gewöhnlich merkt man die Schwierigkeit nicht, weil man nicht einmal mit Leidenschaft, sondern mit einer bequemen Oberflächlichkeit denkt. Die Ausnahme dagegen denkt das Allgemeine mit energischer Leidenschaft. (Kierkegaard, 1909: 200–201)

There are several significant differences in the passage that Schmitt seems to have quoted and the passage in the translation of Kierkegaard's work. Schmitt does not indicate that there are several sentences in the original that he omits nor does he note it by ellipses. He omits some words and changes punctuation. Finally, he ignores that fact that there is a new paragraph where he has a continuous one.

There are no grounds to criticize the length of the quotation nor its placement. But there are several grounds for a genuine critique of Schmitt's use of this quotation. First, unlike much of the reverences in *Politische Theologie,* Schmitt refrains from identifying the author of this quotation. The only indication of its author was Schmitt's indication that it was from "a Protestant theologian" ("ein protestantischer Theologe"). There is another hint when Schmitt indicated that this stemmed from the nineteenth century. With a fair amount of research, the quotation is found in the Danish theologian Soren Kierkegaard's work *Fear and Trembling (Furcht und Zittern)*. However, it is not from that major work but from "Wiederholung" which is found at the end of that volume. "Furcht und Zittern" takes up more than half of the volume (3–116) while "Wiederholung" appears to take up the rest (117–204). A closer examination reveals that this is not as straightforward as it seems because "Wiederholung" is composed of two different sections. The first section is not given a separate title and runs from page 117 to 163. The second section has its own title "Wiederholung" and covers pages 163 to 204. But this does not really explain how the work is set up. The subtitle of the whole work is "An attempt in experimental psychology" ("Ein Versuch in der experimentierenden Psychologie") and the author is listed as "Constantin Constantius." Kierkegaard's choice of name is instructive because the notion of the "constant" as reflective in the name is juxtaposed with the notion of change as indicated by the reference to the Eleatics who denied the possibility of change (Kierkegaard, 1909: 119). There is a consistent form in the first unnamed section and into the section "Wiederholung." But on page 171 Kierkegaard begins to couch his work in the form of letters. These are each addressed to "mein stiller Mitwisser" ("my quiet co-knower") and begins on August 15 and ends on May 31. Then there is nothing until "August 1843" and it is not addressed to "mein stiller Mitwisser" but "to his well-born master R.R., the real reader of this book" ("An Sein Wohlgeboren herrn R.R. den wirklichen Leser dieses Buches") (Kierkegaard, 1909: 198). The author notes that his work does not fit in any typical category and is likely to disappoint most readers.

Schmitt did not address any of Kierkegaard's general points; instead, Schmitt wants to emphasize the superiority of the exception over the general. It seems as if this quotation makes his case, but there are several factors which undercut Schmitt's claim. First, Schmitt's quotation is misleading because he gives this as an uninterrupted whole. However, it is composed of two passages which are separated by several lengthy sentences. The first one indicates that the exception gain is value from the general. The general is polemical against the exception. If it was not against the general, then it would have no power. If it lacked this power, then it would have no value. It would serve the exception well if it did not oppose the general too early. The sinner certainly does not know in the beginning that he is worth more than the 99 just individuals. In contrast, the sinner will only know God's wrath. But the second point is also important as this omitted portion helps indicate. Far from being worthless, the general has both intrinsic as well as additional worth. This is underscored because the exception and the general are engaged in a dialectic (Kierkegaard, 1909: 199–200). Although Schmitt is correct to use Kierkegaard's writing to help further his point about the importance of the exception, his use is sloppy scholarship and is even misleading.

Concluding Comments

Schmitt has spent the entire Chapter I explaining the definition of sovereignty that he gave as the opening sentence. Far from being a simple definition, he supplied not only a considerable historical background but juxtaposed his preference for the exception in contrast to those who preferred the normal. But he also insisted that there are epistemological, legal, and interests that the exception can provide which the normal cannot. The normal cannot teach us anything because it is normal—it is mind-numbingly repetitious. The normal cannot give us anything juridical about the exception because it lies outside the boundaries of the law. The normal is boring because of its repetition. Finally, it is worth repeating that Schmitt agreed with Max Weber that the sovereign is not a matter of what he is as it is a matter of what he does. But Schmitt disagreed with Weber that domination was important because of the physical power to enforce obedience; instead, it was the authority to decide. "The sovereign is he who decides over the state of exception." ("Souverän ist, wer über den Ausnahmezustand entscheidet." (Schmitt, 1923: 5, 1934: 11, 2015: 13).

References

Adair-Toteff, C. (2025). *Dictatorial Power and the State of Exception. The Controversial Article 48 in the Weimar Constitution. 1919–1933*. Routledge.

Bodin, J. (1992) *On Sovereignty. Four Chapters from The Six Books of the Commonwealth* (J. H. Franklin, Ed. and Trans.). Cambridge University Press.

Dreier, H. (2021). *ad Hans Kelsen. Rechtspositivist und Demokrat*. Europäische Verlagsanstalt.

Grimm, Jacob und Wilhelm (1854–) *Deutsches Wörterbuch*. Verlag von S. Hirzel. Band 1. A – Biermolke.

Kierkegaard, S. (1909). *Furcht und Zittern. Wiederholung*. Eugen Diederichs. *Gesammelte Werke* Band 3. Zweite, verbesserte Auflage.

Mehring, R. (1992). *Carl Schmitt. zur Einführung*. Junius.

Mehring, R. (2014). *Kriegstechniker des Begriffs. Biographische Studien zu Carl Schmitt*. Mohr Siebeck.

Métall, R. A. (1969). *Hans Kelsen. Leben und Werk. Eine autorisierte Biographie mit vollständigem Werk-und Schrifttumverzeichnis.* Verlag Franz Deuticke.

Noack, P. (1993). *Carl Schmitt: eine Biographie.* Propyläen.

Preuß, H. (2015). *Das Verfassungswerk von Weimar.* Herausgegeben, eingeleitet und erläutert von Detlef Lehnert, Christoph Müller und Dian Schefold. Mohr Siebeck. *Gesammelte Schriften.* Dritter Band.

Schmitt, C. (1923). Soziologie des Souveränitätsbegriffes und politische Theologie. In *Hauptprobleme der Soziologie. Erinnerungsgabe für Max Weber* (pp. 5–35). Herausgegeben von Melchoir Palyi. Verlag von Duncker & Humblot. II. Band.

Schmitt, C. (1928). *Die Diktatur. Von Anfängen des modernen Souveränitätsgedanken bis zum proletarischen Klassenkampf.* Duncker & Humblot. Zweite Auflage, mit einem Anhang: Die Diktatur des Reichspräsidenten nach Art. 48 der Weimarer Verfassung.

Schmitt, C. (1934). *Politische Theologie. Vier Kapitel zur Lehre von der Souveränität.* Verlag von Duncker & Humblot.

Schmitt, C. (2015). *Politische Theologie. Vier Kapitel zur Lehre von der Souveränität.* Duncker & Humblot. Zehnte Auflage.

Schmitt, C. (2016). *Römischer Katholizismus und politische Form.* Klett-Cotta. Sechste, durchgesehene und erweiterte Auflage.

Schuett, R. (2021). *Hans Kelsen's Political Realism.* Edinburgh University Press.

Weber, M. (1994). *Wissenschaft als Beruf/Politik als Beruf.* Herausgegeben von Wolfgang J. Mommsen und Wolfgang Schluchter in Zusammenarbeit mit Birgitt Morgenbrod. J.C.B. Mohr (Paul Siebeck). *Max Weber Gesamtausgabe.* Band I/17.

Weber, M. (2009). *Allgemeine Staatslehre und Politik (Staatssoziologie). Unvollendet. Mit- und Nachschriften 1920.* Herausgegeben von Gangolf Hübinger in Zusammenarbeit mit Andreas Terwey. J.C.B. Mohr (Paul Siebeck). *Max Weber Gesamtausgabe.* Band III/7.

CHAPTER 4

Sovereignty's Problem

Abstract Chapter I of *Politische Theologie* was focused on providing a definition of sovereignty and on offering a history of the concept. Chapter II concentrates on solving problems regarding sovereignty and in confronting Schmitt's contemporaries. The chapter's title reflects the first while the chapter's contents reflect the second. The title can be translated as "The Problem of Sovereignty as the Problem of Legal Form and the Decision" ("Das Problem der Souveränität als Problem der Rechtsform und der Entscheidung.") (Schmitt 1923: 11; Schmitt 1934: 23; Schmitt 2015: 23). Schmitt references a large number of individuals but concentrates on a handful. He focuses particularly on Hans Kelsen and Hugo Krabbe but also on Kurt Wolzendorff. With the exceptions of Bodin and Hobbes, most of the scholars that Schmitt was criticizing in this chapter had published their works within the previous decade.

Keywords Sovereignty's problem · Legal form · Kelsen · Krabbe

Chapter I of *Politische Theologie* was focused on providing a definition of sovereignty and on offering a history of the concept. Chapter II concentrates on solving problems regarding sovereignty and in confronting Schmitt's contemporaries. The chapter's title reflects the first while the

© The Author(s), under exclusive license to Springer Nature   43
Switzerland AG 2025
C. Adair-Toteff, *Schmitt on Sovereignty and the State of Exception*,
Palgrave Studies in Classical Liberalism,
https://doi.org/10.1007/978-3-031-91728-8_4

chapter's contents reflect the second. The title can be translated as "The Problem of Sovereignty as the Problem of Legal Form and the Decision" ("Das Problem der Souveränität als Problem der Rechtsform und der Entscheidung") (Schmitt, 1923: 11, 1934: 23, 2015: 23). Schmitt references a large number of individuals but concentrates on a handful. He focuses particularly on Hans Kelsen and Hugo Krabbe but also on Kurt Wolzendorff. With the exceptions of Bodin and Hobbes, most of the scholars that Schmitt was criticizing in this chapter had published their works within the previous decade.

Chapter II begins with a general observation. Schmitt contends that much of the "state law" ("Staatsrecht") theory and concepts are evaluated by the impression of its political impact. He takes that to imply that it is evaluated by its practical impact and on how much it achieves its practical ends. Schmitt is contrasting what he takes to be the new "sociological" method and he contrasts it with the older "formalistic" method. It is interesting that Schmitt ignores Eugen Ehrlich because Ehrlich was not only one of the early authors of the "sociology of law" ("Rechtssoziologie"), but had engaged with a long-term polemical exchange with Kelsen in the previous decade. Schmitt may have decided to ignore that in order to concentrate on the legal approaches that he thinks are more pertinent. He suggests that one political approach may give rise to several different legal theories. As indicated, his concern is now with contemporary legal concepts and theories. In the editions of *Politische Theologie,* Schmitt immediately moves to the paragraph which discusses the concept of sovereignty. In contrast, the version in the Palyi volume contains a paragraph that is highly interesting. It is interesting because it contains remarks about several thinkers, about the state of investigation, and the lack of attention to Weber's sociological works.[1]

Schmitt begins that particular paragraph by noting that the interest in the literature regarding the legal state has increased dramatically and that it has reached an almost feverish pitch. But there are certain legal scholars who have been dismissed as not being relevant. He is thinking specifically about Erich Kaufmann and his book which was highly critical of

---

[1] Schmitt does not explain why this paragraph is included in this version but is omitted in the book editions. If anything, it helps clarify Schmitt's understanding of the contemporary juridical approaches. It also helps balance some of Schmitt's criticisms of Max Weber's sociology of law.

the formalism of Neo-Kantian legal philosophy. Rather than taking Kaufmann seriously, many of the highly regarded jurists regard his book as little more than "sham fights" ("Spiegelfechtereien"). Although Schmitt will discuss Kurt Wolzendorff in some detail later, here he mentions that Wolzendorff had enough of a scholarly temperament to suggest that what was warranted was a new idea of a state to serve as the root of a new doctrine of the state. Unfortunately, Kaufmann's work was primarily critical so such a positive conception still awaits. Wolzendorff did not provide such a one. Schmitt concludes this special paragraph with the observation that no one has yet to investigate Weber's "juridical construction of concept" ("juristische Begriffsbildung") (Schmitt, 1923: 12). In all three versions, Schmitt includes the following paragraph.

Schmitt contends that the concept of sovereignty is the one which preoccupies most of modern legal theorists. He does not provide much justification for this claim; he does criticize several recent works which had dealt with the concept of sovereignty. Rather than turning to them, Schmitt repeats his objection to the ongoing claim that sovereignty is the highest power. He repeats his assertion that this claim is wrongfully attributed to Bodin and he again suggests that its history has been somewhat misguided. What Schmitt wants to do is to remind his readers that Bodin developed his concept of sovereignty at the time that the absolute principalities were being dissolved and were being replaced with the notion of the modern sovereign state. Schmitt briefly mentions Emer de Vattel but does not discuss either Vattel's theory of sovereignty or his doctrine of international law. Instead, he moves to the German Constitution of 1871. That constitution attempted to distinguish between the sovereignty of the newly unified Germany and the claim of sovereignty by its member states. Schmitt allowed that that constitution tried to finesse that issue by insisting that the member states had their power without admitting that they were sovereign. Regardless whether these discussions took place in the sixteenth, seventeenth, eighteenth, or even nineteenth centuries, they all seemed to employ the same definition: "Sovereignty is the highest, legally independent, and not derivable power." ("Souveränität ist höchste, rechtlich unabhängige, nicht abgeleitete Macht.") (Schmitt, 1923: 12, 1934: 25–26, 2015: 25–26).

As Schmitt had done in Chapter I, here, too, he inveighs against this definition. He admits that it is so general and so vague that it can be easily used by a variety of the new sociological-political groups. But it does not reflect reality; instead, it is something formal—a sign or a signal.

It is infinitely variable which makes it both inordinately useful as well as completely worthless. Its adherents seem to believe that the "highest power" can be regarded in politics as in physics as the strongest cause. But these proponents overlook the fact that the laws of physics do not have a similar counterpart in politics. The laws of physics cannot be ignored and the "highest power" in nature cannot be dismissed. Yet, the "highest power" in the state can be ignored or even be overthrown. The force in nature cannot be resisted but in politics it can. Schmitt strengthens his case by indicating that force and compulsion do not themselves mean anything for law. Power is power and law is law; but they do not necessarily coincide or overlap. Schmitt is not always acknowledged for his wit but his quotation from Rousseau is an indication of his sharpness. He quotes from the first book of the *Contrat social* in which Rousseau noted that force is a physical power but so is the brigand's pistol ("La force est une puissance physique; le pistole que brigand tient est aussi une puissance.") This leads to Schmitt's claim that the fundamental problem of sovereignty is the connection between the factual and the legal in the highest power. This problem is the basis for all of the difficulties in finding a definition of sovereignty that is not composed of "general tautological predicates" ("allgemeinen tautologischen Prädikaten"), but to find a definition that is precise enough to grasp the "juridical essentialness" ("juristisch Wesentlichkeit") of this "fundamental concept of jurisprudence" ("Grundbegriff der Jurisprudenz") (Schmitt, 1923: 13, 1934: 26–27, 2015: 26).

The most recent attempts to find such a definition have tended to be oversimplifications. These attempts have tried to provide a simple solution by insisting on a clear dichotomy; a simple "either-or" ("Entweder-Oder") that will yield a pure sociological contrast or a pure legal one. Schmitt insists that Kelsen has followed this path in two works: "Das Problem der Souveränität und die Theorie des Völkerrechts" (1920) and "Der soziologische und der juristische Staatsbegriff" (1922). Before turning to Schmitt's critique of Kelsen, it may be helpful to mention somethings about Kelsen and Schmitt during the time that Schmitt wrote his work on sovereignty.

Hans Kelsen does not need much of an introduction but it may be helpful to remember that he was a long-established legal scholar and a constitutional expert. By 1922 he had published a number of works on legal thinking and was already formulating his doctrine of "pure law." This was the legal thinking that Schmitt opposed and will be discussed shortly. It is also important to remember that Kelsen was entrusted to write the Austrian Constitution; one which is mostly still in use today. In contrast, with the exception of *Die Diktatur*, Schmitt had published a number of slim volumes. His *Verfassungslehre* was still in the future as was his feud with Kelsen over the German Constitution.

Schmitt suggested that his criticism in *Politische Theologie* was focused on two of Kelsen's works; however, he was really concerned with the one from 1922 (Kelsen, 1920 and Kelsen, 1922). Schmitt makes it seem as if both works were brief essays when in fact they were lengthy books. "Das Problem der Souveränität und die Theorie des Völkerrechts" is 348 pages in volume 4 of *Hans Kelsen Werke* (Kelsen, 2013: 235–572). "Der soziologische und der juristische Staatsbegriff" encompasses 250 pages in volume 7 of the *Hans Kelsen Werke* (Kelsen, 2022: 99–350). To provide a sketch of the length and the complexity of the latter work, one only needs to recognize that that work has four major sections. The first one discussing the sociological concept of the state, the second one focusing on the juridical concept of the state, the third one on the identity of state and law, and the fourth one on the dualism of law and state in light of epistemological criticism. Another indication is that Kelsen investigates the works of more than fifteen scholars. These included sociologists such as Durkheim, Spencer, Tönnies, and Max Weber. It also included legal scholars such as Georg Jellinek, Rudolf Stammler, Edgar Loening, and Gustav Radbruch. Finally, it included philosophers such as Ernst Cassirer, Hans Vaihinger, and of course, Immanuel Kant.[2] This sketch shows that rather than attempting to find a suitable definition of sovereignty, Kelsen intended to separate the empirical from the legal; hence, his concern with the "is-ought" ("Sein-Sollen") distinction.

According to Schmitt the "Sein-Sollen" distinction has a fairly long history. He does not refer to Hume but that may be because his concern is with the distinction only in legal philosophy. He points out that Georg Jellinek and Theodor Kistiakowski had used it. However, they neither employed it to the same degree nor made the distinction so funda-mental to their jurisprudence. Such is not the case with some of the current thinkers and Schmitt has Kelsen in mind. Jellinek and Kistiakowski may have posited the difference between law and sociology but they did not emphasize it. That is because they were still content to have some

---

[2] For a review essay of Band 7 of the *Hans Kelsen Werke*, see Adair-Toteff (2023). For an account of "Der soziologische und der juristische Staatsbegriff" see pages 300–303.

content remain in their legal thinking whereas Kelsen was insisting on pure formality. That implies that "all sociological elements" are kept as far away as possible from law. Kelsen was intent upon doing this in order to construct as system of calculability which is based upon a "basic norm" ("Grundnorm"). But the main difference between Jellinek and Kelsen is that the latter approached the sociology-law distinction with a greater degree of rigor. Schmitt suggests that that such a distinction appears to belong to the nature of a juristic philosophy. But he also declares that it is not at all surprising that Kelsen arrives at his conclusion of a pure law because his whole approach is predicated by the rejection of "reality." In addition, Kelsen rejects any thinking that is outside the "legal order" ("Rechtsordnung"). Schmitt indicates what the state is *not* for Kelsen: it is not the author or the origin of the "legal order." It cannot include any personification of the state. Schmitt then indicates what the state is for Kelsen: it is "a system of deductions which is based upon the final point of deduction and a final basic norm." ("ein System von Zurechnungen auf einen letzten Zurechnungspunkt und eine letzte Grundnorm.") Schmitt draws from this that the state is neither a person nor a power; it is only a method of deduction. In fact, it is the end point of the process of deduction. Finally, in Schmitt's opinion, from a juridical viewpoint, Kelsen's state is identical with its constitution. That means "the unified basic norm" ("der einheitlichen Grundnorm") (Schmitt, 1923: 13–14, 1934: 28–29, 2015: 26–27). In the next two pages Schmitt focuses on at least two terms "Einheit" and "Reinheit." He is not complaining about the terms themselves but he is arguing against the form in which Kelsen uses them. Throughout much of his life, Schmitt promoted "unity" and "purity" but unlike Kelsen, he considered the material conditions of these terms. That meant fusing jurisprudence with politics; Kelsen separated law from politics just as he had separated law from sociology. Schmitt cites Kelsen four times but he provides a page reference only once. The difficulty in locating the particular passage is made even more so by the fact that Schmitt does not provide complete sentences. In addition, Schmitt's interpretation of Kelsen's thinking does not seem like Kelsen in his writings. This is again partly because there is little chance of finding Schmitt's use of Kelsen's phrases and partly because Schmitt questions Kelsen's account. But it is also partly because of the different ideas that "Einheit" and "Reinheit" had for Kelsen and for Schmitt. Kelsen did not attribute much to the notion of "Einheit"; what was more important for him was "Reinheit." "Reinheit" meant far more to Kelsen that the elimination of material factors in law. "Reinheit" was the elimination of fictional and metaphysical factors as well. Kelsen rejected fictional factors because they were hypotheticals; he had in mind Hans Vaihinger's notion of "Als-ob" ("as-if"). Kelsen rejected metaphysical factors whether they were theories of natural law or Hegelian systems.[3] Schmitt does not rely so much on theories of natural law or philosophical systems, but his thinking is predicated on the monarch's absolutism and the "people's will." For Schmitt, both are pure and represent a unity. In the monarchy, it is the indivisible will of the ruler; in the "will of the people" it is the indivisible will of the nation. In his decisionism, the sovereign decrees and the people obey. But these points will not become clearer until later in *Politische Theologie*. Here, Schmitt intends to discredit Kelsen's account so he faults Kelsen for his account of "Einheit," but Kelsen was not referring to a juristic "Einheit" as much as he was referring to the theological accounts of the unity of God and state (Kelsen, 2022: 319–321). Schmitt writes "The great word of this deduction is 'unity'." ("Das große Wort dieser Deduktion ist 'Einheit'.") Yet the term "Deduktion" does not occur in the extensive "Sachregister." Schmitt's references to mathematic mythology and to systematic unity are also absent. Instead, these are basically Schmitt's ideas. Schmitt is on more solid ground when he criticizes Kelsen for a normative jurisprudence because one void of an objective standard of value cannot be regarded as normative without values. Schmitt is again on less solid ground when he insists that it was easy for Kelsen to find "unity and purity" when he had eliminated all of the difficulties. Schmitt concludes his critique of Kelsen by suggesting that Kelsen's methodological efforts, his conceptual sharpness, and his penetrating criticisms are certainly helpful but they do not address the matter itself. Instead, Kelsen remains "in the antechamber of jurisprudence." ("in der Antichambre der Jurisprudenz.") (Schmitt, 1923: 15, 1934: 30–31, 2015: 28–29).[4]

As I have suggested, Schmitt was not always accurate in citing his opponents and he was not totally fair even to those he tended to agree

---

[3] These theses are extremely important and several Kelsen experts have explored them. But Kelsen's rejections and the experts' investigations are much removed from the focus of my account.

[4] In the Palyi collection the sentence does not end with this phrase but continues after a comma with a reference to Erich Kaufmann's critic of Neo-Kantian legal philosophy. Schmitt praises Kaufmann for pointing out the one-dimensionality of this manner of thinking and for showing how problematic it is (Schmitt 1923: 15).

with. Both of these approaches will be shown again later in this chapter and the following two. But Schmitt was adamantly opposed to Kelsen and it is with justification that Kelsen and Schmitt have been regarded as antipodes. Schmitt was fundamentally against Kelsen's pluralism and tolerance. He decried democracy and favored a type of authoritarianism. By focusing on Kelsen's pure legal philosophy, Schmitt could still discount Kelsen's political leanings. Having dispatched Kelsen, Schmitt turns to dispense with Hugo Krabbe.[5]

Hugo Krabbe (1857–1936) spent most of his life in Leiden—he was born there, he graduated from its university, and taught there for almost two decades. He published his works in Dutch but two of them were translated into German. These were the two that Schmitt referred to: the first is *Die Lehre der Rechtssouveränität. Beitrag zur Staatslehre* (*The Doctrine of Legal Sovereignty. An Essay on the Doctrine of State*) which was published in 1906 while he was a professor at the university in Groningen. (Krabbe, 1906). The second is *Die Moderne Staats-Idee* (*The Modern Idea of State*). Schmitt suggests that the first book is a second edition in 1919. Yet this is misleading because Krabbe indicated in the "Vorwort" to *Die Moderne Staats-Idee* that the new work was a response to the criticisms and comments regarding the 1906 book. Both were written in his "mother language" (Dutch) and he wanted the first book translated to reach more readers. The second book was to be published in 1915 but was delayed because of the war. He also wrote a work that appeared in 1917 and that *Die Moderne Staats-Idee* is based upon the 1915 and the 1917 Dutch books (Krabbe, 1919: V). It is unclear how and why Schmitt overlooked Krabbe's clarification.

Schmitt's animosity against Kelsen is apparent in his opening comments on Krabbe. Schmitt suggests that Kelsen's demand in

---

[5] Kelsen provides two important points which should be kept in mind when considering Schmitt's criticism of Kelsen and Schmitt's comments on Krabbe. Schmitt will suggest that far from being original, Kelsen's ideas were prefigured in Krabbe's writings. But in the "Vorrede" to *Das Problem der Souveränität und die Theorie des Völkerrechts* Kelsen explained that he began work on it in 1915 and in 1916 it was mostly finished. However, his military service forced the publication delay until after the war. The second point is far from ignoring Krabbe's work, he regarded Krabbe's *Die moderne Staats-Idee* as a "beautiful book" ("schönes Buch") (Kelsen 2013: 267–268). While the 1919 book appeared too late for Kelsen to use, he devoted nine pages to Krabbe's *Die Lehre von der Rechtssouveränität*. Kelsen's comments are highly interesting but cannot be discussed here (Kelsen 2013: 292–301).

"Problem der Souveränität" that the concept of sovereignty must be radically reconstructed" was not an original conclusion. Instead, it was the "old denial of the state" ("alte Negierung des Staates") in favor of the law. It also ignored the problem of "actualizing law" ("Rechtsverwirklichung"). Rather than being the originator of this thesis, Schmitt insisted that it was found in the first edition of Krabbe's work and then in a clearer formulation in the 1919 version. A glance at the two show some overlap but considerable differences. Some of the differences are statistical: the 1906 book has 254 pages and is comprised of six chapters, include the first one of six pages. In contrast, the 1919 book has 311pages and is comprised of ten chapters. There are substantial differences: the 1906 book focused on the doctrine of legal sovereignty while the 1919 book was devoted to the idea of the state. Despite the claim that the 1919 book dealt with the modern state, some of the early chapters focused on the state in history. In contrast, the 1906 book is almost exclusively devoted to contemporary theories of the sovereignty of the state. Another difference is that "force" ("Gewalt") is a prominent topic in the earlier work where it hardly appears in the later one. The major overlap is with the twin notions of law and state. It is with these two notions that Schmitt directs his attention.

Schmitt claims that what is clearer in the 1919 book is that Krabbe contended that sovereignty was something that the law had, and not the state. Schmitt again indicates that the idea that Kelsen was the originator of the identification of the state and the legal order is misleading because it was found first in Krabbe's book. The result was the same; the only difference was that Kelsen relied on his German Neo-Kantian theory of knowledge to arrive at the same conclusion that the Dutch scholar Krabbe had reached earlier in *Die Lehre der Rechtssouveränität*. It is not exactly clear which book Schmitt is citing, but he does cite the correct page in *Die Moderne Staats-Idee*. The passage that he quotes is "The doctrine of the 'sovereignty of law' is, depending on which way one wants to take it, either the description of a actual existing condition, or a pure postulate which should be striving after this actualization." ("Der Lehre von der 'Rechtssouveränität' ist, je nachdem es nehmen will, entweder die Beschreibung eines wirklich bestehenden Zustandes, oder rein Postulat, nach dessen Verwirklichung gestrebt werden soll.") (Krabbe, 1919: 39; Schmitt, 1923: 15–16, 1934: 31, 2015: 29). Schmitt then quotes from four passages without indicating which ones, then he mentions page 75. Schmitt claims that there Krabbe was engaged in an investigation of the sociology of "domination" ("Herrschaft"). However, Krabbe indicated that he was dissatisfied with the sociological investigation into the various forms in which social powers manifest themselves. Krabbe specifically points to Von Wieser's *Recht und Macht* (1910). Krabbe's comment occurs in Krabbe's discussion of the relationship between law and power and is also concerned with Jellinek's "'ethical minimum'" (Krabbe, 1919: 75, 77–78, 109–112, 138). In fact, much of Krabbe's book is a commentary on Jellinek and he mentions his agreement with Kelsen about the foundation of law in norms (Krabbe, 1919: 45). Schmitt does not mention any of these points; instead, he mentions Krabbe's distinction between private and civil law and then insists that Krabbe is convinced that the law should have power and not the state ("Nicht der Staat, sondern das Recht soll die Macht haben.") The page Schmitt lists does not indicate this at all; rather, it is a discussion of the bureaucrat as a private person (Krabbe, 1919: 138). Schmitt does provide a lengthy quotation and much of it is accurate. Krabbe was explaining the notion of power and its execution. However, Schmitt lists it as one page when it began on one and ended on the one he lists. More importantly, he alters the final sentence. His reads: "Nicht also in der Anwendung von Gesetzen oder Wahrnemung irgendwelcher öffentlicher Intereressen" while Krabbe's is "Nicht also in der Anwendung von Exekution oder Strafe, nicht in der Arbeit der Richter oder des Heeres und der Polizei." Krabbe continued by listing all of the interests that the state has in everyday life: post and telegrams, railroads and mines, etc. His point is in the "revelation of the idea of the state" (Krabbe, 1919: 254–255). It is noteworthy that the phrase "öffentlicher Interessen" occurs a few pages later. Schmitt provides another citation but he does not indicate that it is only a partial sentence. Because Schmitt begins it in a sentence the "Nicht" is capitalized. More importantly, by taking it out of context Schmitt can employ it to bolster his claim. But Krabbe's point is a continuation of his comments on bureaucracy and the construction of law. Finally, Krabbe was contrasting the modern idea of the state with the absolute monarchy where the monarch both produced and enforced the law whereas it is separated in the modern state into the legislative and executive groups. But Schmitt maintains that Krabbe believed that "The state has only the task to 'form' the law, that means the determination of the legal value of interests." ("Der Staat hat nur die Aufgabe, das Recht zu 'biden', das heißt die Feststellung des Rechtswertes der Interessen.") (Krabbe, 1919: 260–261; Schmitt, 1923: 16–17, 1934: 33, 2015: 31).

Schmitt declares that because of his concern with interests, Krabbe differentiates himself from formal Kantianism and he suggests that that brings Krabbe closer to those who fought against the authoritative state—people such as Hugo Preuß.

The amount of space devoted to Preuß is rather minimal. It is unclear why Schmitt included him, other than his dislike of Preuß' liberalism. Schmitt is more concerned with some ideas from Otto von Gierke. The two that interest Schmitt are the claim that the law is the final stamp and the claim that the law has the final value. This allegedly links Gierke with Krabbe. Rather than pursuing that linkage, Schmitt turns to the writings by Kurt Wolzendorff (Schmitt, 1923:17, 1934: 34–35, 2015: 32).

Kurt Wolzendorff (1882–1921) was born in Nassau and studied at Marburg. He earned his doctorate in 1905 with a dissertation on the use of force by police. He then "habilitated" in 1913 becoming an "extraordinary professor" at Königsberg in 1917. He succeeded Edgar Loening at Halle in 1917. He was a member of the German delegation to Versailles in 1919. Wolzendorff had published a number of brief works when he unexpectedly died in March 1921 of a lung infection. Schmitt makes references to several of these writings but the one he concentrates on is one of Wolzendorff's final essays "Der reine Staat." Schmitt does so primarily because in this work Wolzendorff attempted to describe the conditions necessary for a new political epoch. But Schmitt might have been inclined to consider this work because Wolzendorff complimented Schmitt's *Politische Romantik*. In a footnote Wolzendorff wrote "On the concept and essence of 'political romantic' see the impressive and deep study by Carl Schmitt-Dorotić which appeared in 1919 under the same title"[6] (Wolzendorff, 1920: 223, note 1).

In "Der reine Staat" Wolzendorff argued that the Weimar Constitution was a flawed document because it lacked clarity and contained contradictions, especially in the second part which dealt with fundamental rights and duties. Because of these, he thought it necessary to inaugurate a "new epoch of state life" ("neuen Epoche des Staatslebens") one which emphasized the fact that the state was life and as such was incomplete. But he insisted that there was a fundamental tension between humans and the state; between freedom and the state (Wolzendorff, 1920: 199–200). He complained that the socialists believed in a lifeless planning and he

---

[6] "Ueber Begriff und Wesen der 'politische Romantik' vgl. Die 1919 unter diesem Titel erschienene feinsinnige und tiefgründige Studie von Carl Schmitt-Dorotić."

argued that the democrats believed in a lifeless theory, so it was necessary to construct a new theory of the state. He likens the year 1920 to the great time of Prussia. That was the time in the early part of the nineteenth century when Stein, Hardenberg, Scharnhorst, Boyen, and others reformed the state, education, and the military (Wolzendorff, 1920: 207). He thought that the best way to proceed was to eliminate many functions of the state and to reduce it to its essential duties. That is why he refers to his project as "The Pure State" ("Der reine Staat") (Wolzendorff, 1920: 209, 211, 217–218). For Wolzendorff, the essence of the modern state is the "police power" ("Polizeigewalt") and is necessary to maintain order (Wolzendorff, 1920: 220). He granted that scholars have considered the state as ideology, morality, culture, power, and social justice and while each of these is part of the state, none of them are the state. He claimed that the contemporary emphasis on "experience" ("Erlebnis") is particularly problematic: "That is real political Romantic." ("Das ist echte politische Romantik.") (Wolzendorff, 1920: 222–223). In *politische Romantik* Schmitt had complained that it was the liberal inclination toward "revolution, Rousseauism, unfettered subjectivism" (Schmitt, 1982: 33). For Wolzendorff, the opposite of political romanticism is just as bad and he objected to the formalism of modern law. He did not name Kelsen but he contended such pure law theories reduce the state to an abstraction. As such it is at odds with the "German spirit" ("deutschen Geistes")—the state is a part of the life of the "Volk" (Wolzendorff, 1920: 225–228). Given all of this, it is difficult to understand what Schmitt found objectionable.

Schmitt begins with a rather positive assessment of Wolzendorff's "Der reine Staat" and he has an accurate understanding of that essay. He notes that Wolzendorff believed that the state needs the law and the law needs the state and that its most basic principle is force. Schmitt agrees with him that this force is not just the force of some compulsion but is developed into something ripe. But Schmitt suggested that such a historical process often leads to the discussion of dictatorship. He does not pursue that idea but instead correctly assesses Wolzendorff's "pure state" as one which has been reduced to maintaining order. He writes "Wolzendorff's pure state is a state which has been reduced to its function of order." ("Wolzendorffs reiner Staat ist ein Staat, der sich auf seine Ordnungsfunktion beschränkt.") Schmitt adds that that means that all law is reduced to laws ensuring order and that limits the state to that of a guardian. The state is not something that produces but guards it is "'guardian, not as giver'" ("'Hüter, nicht als Gebieter'"). Schmitt adds that this does not reduce the state to a "blind servant" because the state is the final decisive guarantor.[7]

Schmitt's criticism of Wolzendorff rests on the fact that he regards Wolzendorff as one the most recent proponents of a theory of community and a democratic one. He compares Wolzendorff with Krabbe and he thinks that the former has taken the theory a further step. That is why Schmitt regarded Wolzendorff's most recent work as so important. A reader may not be attuned to the points that Schmitt is raising but his use of the word "decision" ("Entscheidung") should help clarify them. But it is Schmitt who emphasizes the importance of "decision," not Wolzendorff. Schmitt recognizes this because he faults him for placing too much value on "'social-psychological phenomena'" ("'sozial-psychologischen Phänomen'") and for stressing the "historical-political life" ("'historisch-politischen Lebens'"). In Schmitt's view, Wolzendorff was too preoccupied with particularities and not concerned with the general importance of making decisions. Instead, Wolzendorff reduced the state to a "formation of life" ("Lebensgestaltung"). Schmitt conceded that this made the state into something between that which could be predictable and that which was little more than something aesthetic (Schmitt, 1923: 18, 1934: 36–37, 2015: 33–34).

Schmitt turns his attention to Weber's "sociology of law" ("Rechtssoziologie"). Before turning to Schmitt's comments, it is helpful to place Weber's "Rechtssoziologie" in its proper context. Weber's "Rechtssoziologie" is only one portion of his *Wirtschaft und Gesellschaft*. This work has a long history of debate and cannot be discussed here. But it is crucial to note that only the first part (that means the part that Weber wrote last) was published in Weber's lifetime. The second part (meaning the part that Weber had written earlier) was compiled and edited by Marianne Weber with the assistance of Melchoir Palyi. The main body of *Wirtschaft und*

---

[7] Schmitt (1923: 18, 1934: 36, 2015: 33). Here Schmitt has put together a number of phrases from different parts of Wolzendorff's essay without indicating that he has omitted some words which alter his meaning. The phrase "blinder Diener" appears on page 219, but the "Hüter, nicht Gebieter" does not occur until the final page—229. Furthermore, the phrase is "because it is the state as guardian, not as giver of human value." ("weil sie den Staat als Hüter, nicht als Gebieter menschlicher Wert." Finally, the guarantor passage is "that means, to rule as the responsible and final deciding guarantor of the law." ("d.h. als verantwortlicher und letztentscheidender Garant des Rechts zu walten.") (Wolzendorff 1920: 220).

Gesellschaft is based upon notes and manuscripts that Weber had written sometime between 1910 and 1913. As such, they do not reflect Weber's later thinking nor are they in the form in which he would have wanted them to appear. In addition, the "Rechtssoziologie" is huge—it is found between pages 386 and 512 (Weber, 1922: 386–512).[8] In light of these points, it was somewhat misleading of Schmitt to fault Weber for ideas that he might not have had in the manner that Schmitt chose to express.

Schmitt begins his critique of Weber by noting that the unwarranted emphasis on the notion of form in philosophy has been intensified in sociology and jurisprudence. He lists the various types of form: "Rechtsform, techniche Form, aesthetische Form und schließlich der Form der transzendalen Philosophie" which designate different things. In a similar manner, Weber differentiates among three different concepts of form in his "Rechtssoziologie." Schmitt maintains that these three can be considered as (1) legal form, (2) substantial form, and (3) rational form. The first and third reflect Schmitt's own terminological choices; the second is an expression of what Schmitt writes but is not a term that Weber actually uses. How much this reflects Weber's own legal sociology is difficult to determine because Schmitt only provides one general reference.[9] In regards to point 1) Schmitt suggests that it is Weber's distinction between the legal content and the legal form. This is supposed to refer to Weber's notion of regulation but contains a normative component.[10] Point 2) is more important in that Schmitt indicates the substance of Weber's legal form. In this sense it refers to something that is rational, expertly determined, and predictable. This is indeed Weber's conception but there is no reference to such a phrase in the "Sachregister" (Weber, 2010). Schmitt has a fairly good understanding of the conception of law that Weber learned as a student and practiced as an expert. Schmitt

---

[8] For a brief account of how *Wirtschaft und Gesellschaft* was assembled and published see "Allgemeine Hinweise der Herausgeber der Max Weber-Gesamtausgabe" (1999). Weber (2010: VII–XVI). For a lengthy account of Weber's "Recht" see the massive "Einleitung" in the same volume. Weber (2010: 1–133).

[9] Rechtssoziologie II § I. This manner of citing is not accurate. In the Table of Contents (Inhalt) Kapitel VII. Rechtssozioloie (Wirtschaft und Recht). Does not contain a "II" but has 8 §s. It seems that Schmitt probably has in mind § 2. Furthermore, § 2 runs sixteen pages. Weber (1922: 396–412).

[10] Schmitt quotes Weber as saying "kausale Komponente des Einverständishandelns" but I cannot find such a phrase in the text nor any indication of something similar in the index.

does not cite Weber but is accurate in construing Weber's legal thinking by emphasizing that which is regular, equal, and calculable. Schmitt is also correct to note that Weber insisted that such an educated, expert judiciary was necessary for economic transactions. He is not really over-stating Weber's position when he maintains that such an educated and professional bureaucracy is crucial for the ideal of a smooth functioning economy (Schmitt, 1923: 21–22, 1934: 38, 2015: 34). It is clear that Schmitt does not approve of such a legal system because of its boring regularity and its insistence on the general.

The next several topics are directly related to Weber. The immediate one is Schmitt's continued criticism of Neo-Kantian legal theories. He explains that there is no particular need to discuss them in general, there is only the need to point out their "precision" and their "history of points of purposefulness" ("Zweckmäßigkeitsgeschichtspunkten"). Schmitt maintains that Neo-Kantians can appreciate the technical precision of legal commands because they are similar to military orders. However, Neo-Kantians reject that as failing to be a "legal ideal" ("Rechtsideal"). But Schmitt suggests that Neo-Kantian pure law fails to reflect reality.

The other topic is also related to Weber because it involves Emil Lask (1875–1914). Lask was a student of Heinrich Rickert and is regarded as a Neo-Kantian. He was, however, close to Weber and was influenced by Weber's legal thinking. Schmitt's inclusion here is somewhat perplexing. He notes Lask's philosophy of categories and that it contains an intriguing notion of subject/object. But it is unclear why he chose to focus on Lask's "Kategorienlehre" and not his contribution to the "Festschrift" for Kuno Fischer. In his "Rechtsphilosophie" Lask provided a relatively clear and rather concise account of the tension between the metaphysics of natural law and the anti-metaphysics of positive law. Lask placed great emphasis on the latest Neo-Kantian legal philosophy which combined the individualistic embrace of freedom with the accommodations of modern social life. The reliance on Weber is further manifested in Lask's emphasis on methodology, his use of ideal types, and his claim that law is a "cultural science" ("Kulturwissenschaft") (Lask, 1907: 284–285, 297–300). It is also odd that Schmitt ignored that work because Lask discussed Jellinek and Kistiakowski and their "normative juridical doctrine" ("juristische Sollenslehre") (Lask, 1907: 305). What is not peculiar is that Schmitt objected to each of these types of legal thinking because they all emphasized the objectivity of law. They all make law general whereas Schmitt's entire thesis has been the importance of the specific individual—the one who decides.

Schmitt returns to writings of Kelsen, Krabbe, and Preuß. It is not entirely clear how Schmitt thinks that Kelsen contradicts himself. On the one hand, he insists that Kelsen's Neo-Kantianism rests upon the "subjectivist concept of form" ("subjektivistischen Formbegriff") and on the other hand he contends that Kelsen's claim for objectivity is not much more than Hegelian collectivity. But Schmitt fails to provide any evidence for the latter claim. Schmitt is on more solid ground when he maintains that Kelsen minimized all that is personal and rests his legal order upon the impersonal validity of an impersonal norm (Schmitt, 1923: 22, 1934: 39–40, 2015: 35).

Krabbe, Preuß, and Kelsen may have different approaches to the notion of sovereignty but all of these are based upon claims of objectivity. Furthermore, the inclination to shed jurisprudence of everything personal and in different ways ensure that legal thinking is totally impersonal. This is true for all of their thinking and it is especially applicable to their individual theories of state. However, Schmitt argues that they misunderstand that the state is not something abstract but is the person who makes decisions and commands. He writes "Personality and command obviously belong together." ("Persönlichkeit und Befehl gehören sie offenbar zusammen.") Kelsen misunderstands this when he suggests that the idea of the personal command is the specific error of the doctrine of the sovereignty of the state. He also errs in condemning such a doctrine as being "subjectivistic" and that it is the "negation" of legality. That is because Kelsen objects to the subjectiveness of command because it attempts to replace the "objectively accepted norm" ("objektiv geltenden Norm").

Krabbe is seems to be problematic because he connects the opposition between the personal and the impersonal with the opposition between the concrete and individual—as opposed to the universal and the general. This apparent confusion is prompted in part because Schmitt used two words in German which often can have the same meaning: "Allgemein" and "Generell." But it is also prompted in part because Schmitt chose to use "Allgemein" instead of the word for abstract ("Abstrakt"). That opposition is less between the concrete and the general than it is greater between the concrete and the abstract. This is highlighted by Schmitt's contrast between two other sets: 1) between official and legal principle and authority and "quality" and 2) between person and idea. He suggests that the personal command has been transformed into the factual validity of the abstract norm. For Preuß and Krabbe, any traces of the personal in law are remainders from the era of absolute monarchies. Schmitt suggests that these rejections of everything personal reflects a massive misunderstanding about the nature of legal decisions (Schmitt, 1923: 23, 1934: 40, 2015: 36).

Schmitt spends most of the remainder of Chapter II in clarifying the nature of legal decisions. He uses some form of the word for "decision" more than twenty times within two pages. He notes that a legal decision is an idea that is within jurisprudence and that it still confronts reality. In a similar vein a legal norm still has to conform to an actual concrete situation. Schmitt stresses that the situation is independent of the legal norm and that the situation has much more importance. He is suggesting that scholars are deluding themselves in thinking that abstract legal principles are somehow far more superior to the actual concrete occurrence. Schmitt acknowledges that legal thinking is preoccupied with generalities and that generality fosters predictability. So, it attempts to subsume the decision under the "general universality" ("generellen Allgemeinheit"). In reality, there is a transformation from the supposed superiority of the abstract to the real power of the concrete. It is the individual person and the concrete instance that are determinative. This is a point that Schmitt is convinced that Krabbe ignored (Schmitt, 1923, 1934, 2015: 37).

Ignorance can be the cause of erroneous decisions. But given Schmitt's emphasis on the importance of decisions, the idea of a decision made in error is an uncomfortable notion. This may explain much of this sections lack of clarity. It is not clear what he means by pure juristic nature nor is it evident who he is thinking about. But things improve when Schmitt moves to discuss the age-old connection between law and authority. He refers to John Locke without indicating which work, much less what page. But his point in clear and that is that Locke is well within the legal tradition when he contended that law has authority because it is impersonal. This follows the contrast with the personal command.

Schmitt begins the conclusion of Chapter II by insisting that there are two types of "juristic scholarliness" ("juristischer Wissenschaftlichkeit"). There are those who contend that authority and truth are connected and then there are those who believe that they are separate. He believes that Hobbes was the one who best expressed the latter with his claim "Autoritas, non veritas facit legem." Schmitt contends further that Hobbes' opposition between "autoritas" and "veritas" is far more radical than Friedrich Julius Stahl's claim "Authority, not majority" ("Autorität, nicht Majorität"). He does not dwell on it, but it is revealing that as much as Schmitt rejects the elevation of the majority in democracies, he is more concerned about the power of the individual ruler. Hobbes did not regard his theory as "decisionism," but Schmitt does. As indicated earlier, Schmitt frequently takes liberties with other thinkers' ideas and manipulates the words of other scholars. But here Schmitt accurately reflects much of Hobbes' philosophy. Hobbes insisted on the ruler's power and he rejected the notion of abstract legal principles. Hobbes was too influenced by the natural sciences to believe that there could be similar principles governing human behavior. Hobbes was too astute to believe that human beings interacted in any ways other than being motivated by passions. Fear and pride drove people; principles were fine but could not fundamentally motivate people. Schmitt is also correct to emphasize Hobbes' notion of "power"; but Hobbes did not employ the word in the sense of "Macht" as he did in the sense of "force." Schmitt notes that Hobbes used the English word "power" and the Latin term "potesta" but he rightly noted that the word meant the power to force or to compel subjection. Again, he utilizes Hobbes' own words from *Leviathan* "For Subjection, Command, Right and Power are accidents, not of Powers but of Persons" (Hobbes, 1992: 378). Hobbes was speaking about the hierarchy of the spiritual over the earthly, the eternal over the temporal, but Schmitt's citing of this passage from Part 3 of the *Leviathan* is still appropriate. What is also appropriate is Schmitt's assertion that it is remarkable that Hobbes, who was so heavily influenced by the universality found in the natural sciences, would insist on the primacy of the personal in his legal philosophy. Schmitt refers to Hobbes' insistence that he was intent of capturing the reality of "social life" ("gesellschaftlcihen Lebens") as he was capturing the reality of nature. Schmitt continues with the observation that Hobbes seemed not to be fully aware that the juristic reality that exists is not the actual reality that was needed. The form that he sought exists in the concrete instance and that the key question about that is the question of who decides and that is based upon reality. Schmitt concludes the final paragraph of Chapter II with the assertion that this decision is not connected to the "aprior emptiness of the transcendental form" ("apriorische Leerheit der transzendentalen Form") and is not the "form of technical precision" ("Form der technischen Präzision"). It is not that because that has "an essentially objective, impersonal purposeful interest" ("ein wesentlich sachliches, unpersönliches Zweckinteresse"). Finally, a decision does not recognize the form of aesthetic formation (Schmitt, 1923: 26, 1934: 46, 2015: 40). Schmitt's Chapter II is not an easy one to explain. He assumes that the reader is well-aware of the writings of the numerous authors that he references. He also assumes that his reader has a firm grounding in the history of philosophy and has more than just a working knowledge of Hobbes' philosophy. He also assumes that his reader has a rather good grasp of the contemporary legal thinking. Finally, by leaving aside specific page numbers he makes it harder to identify the passage that Schmitt is apparently referring to. But maybe Schmitt's purpose is not to provide a scholarly defense of his decisionism, but to make a compelling political case.

References

Adair-Toteff, C. (2023). Hans Kelsen and sociology. *Journal of Classical Sociology, 23*(2), 299–305.

Hobbes, T. (1992) *Leviathan* (R. Tuck, Ed.). Cambridge University Press.

Krabbe, H. (1919). *Die moderne Staats-Idee.* Martinus Nijhoff. Deutsche, zweite vermehrter Ausgabe.

Kelsen, H. (1920). Das Problem der Souveränität und die Theorie des Völkerrechts. In Kelsen 2013 (pp. 235–572).

Kelsen, H. (1922). Der soziologische und der juristische Staatsbegriff. In Kelsen 2022 (pp. 99–350).

Kelsen, H. (2013). *Hans Kelsen Werke.* Herausgegeben von Matthias Jestaedt. In Kooperation mit dem Hans Kelsen-Institut. Mohr Siebeck. Band 4. *Veröffentlichte Schriften 1918–1920.*

Kelsen, H. (2022). *Hans Kelsen Werke.* Herausgegeben von Matthias Jestaedt. In Kooperation mit dem Hans Kelsen-Institut. Mohr Siebeck. Band 7. *Veröffentlichte Schriften 1921–1923.*

Krabbe, H. (1906). *Die Lehre der Rechtssouveränität. Beitrag zur Staatslehre.* Verlag von J.B. Wolters.

Lask, E. (1907). Rechtsphilosophie. In *Die Philosophie im Beginn des zwanzigsten Jahrhunderts. Festschrift für Kuno Fischer.* Herausgegeben von W. Windelband (pp. 269–320). Carl Winter's Universitätsbuchhandlung. Zweite verbesserte und das Kapitel Naturphilosophie erweiterte Auflage.

Schmitt, C. (1923). Soziologie des Souveränitätsbegriffes und politische Theologie. In *Hauptprobleme der Soziologie. Erinnerungsgabe für Max Weber.* Herausgegeben von Melchoir Palyi (pp. 5–35). Verlag von Duncker & Humblot. II. Band.

Schmitt, C. (1934). *Politische Theologie. Vier Kapitel zur Lehre von der Souveränität.* Duncker & Humblot.

Schmitt, C. (1982). *Politische Romantik.* Duncker & Humblot. Vierte Auflage.

Schmitt, C. (2015). *Politische Theologie. Vier Kapitel zur Lehre von der Souveränität.* Duncker & Humblot. Zehnte Auflage.

Weber, M. (1922). *Wirtschaft und Gesellschaft.* Verlag von J.C.B. Mohr (Paul Siebeck).

Weber, M. (2010). *Wirtschaft und Gesellschaft. Die Wirtschaft und die gesellschaftlichen Ordnung und Mächte. Nachlaß.* Teilbad 3: Recht. Herausgegeben von Werner Gephart und Siegfried Hermes. J.C.B. Mohr (Paul Siebeck). *Max Weber Gesamtausgabe.* Band I/23-3.

Wolzendorff, K. (1920). Der Reine Staat.Skizze zum Problem einer neuen Staatsepoche. *Zeitschrift für die gesamte Staatswissenschaft/Journal of Institutional and Theoretical Economics.* Band 75, Heft 1/2 (1920) (pp. 199–229).

CHAPTER 5

Sovereignty's Theology

Abstract In Chapter III Carl Schmitt begins to lay out his positive theory, but even here much of it is negative and critical. He accuses many legal scholars from the nineteenth and twentieth centuries of being polemical. Yet, a similar complaint might be said about Schmitt regarding the two previous chapters as well as the one now under examination. Schmitt's target is again mainly Hans Kelsen, but Hugo Krabbe and Hugo Preuß are also criticized. Even Max Weber's sociology of the state is found to be defective. In each of these cases, the scholar has committed a cardinal offense; that is, to eliminate theology from law. This is a cardinal offense for two reasons: it obscures the history of legal thinking and it distorts the nature of law. Schmitt adds another discipline to the two he has already addressed and that is philosophy. Whereas the first two chapters were focused on law and sociology; Chapter III includes those to and adds philosophy and theology. Schmitt mentions Hobbes again, but he also includes René Descartes, Gottfried Wilhelm Leibniz, and Jean-Jacques Rousseau. Despite the introduction of theology and philosophy, politics is lurking in the background. Hence, Schmitt's Chapter III has the title "Politische Theologie."

Keywords Sovereignty theory · Kelsen · Weber · Krabbe · Max Weber · Preuß

C. Adair-Toteff, *Schmitt on Sovereignty and the State of Exception*, Palgrave Studies in Classical Liberalism, https://doi.org/10.1007/978-3-031-91728-8_5

In Chapter III Carl Schmitt begins to lay out his positive theory, but even here much of it is critical and even negative. He accuses many legal scholars from the nineteenth and twentieth centuries of being polemical. Yet, a similar complaint might be made about Schmitt himself regarding the two previous chapters as well as this one now under examination. Schmitt's target is again mainly Hans Kelsen, but Hugo Krabbe and Hugo Preuß are also criticized. Even Max Weber's sociology of the state is found to be defective. In each of these cases, the scholar has committed a cardinal offense; that is, to have eliminated theology from law. This is a cardinal offense for two reasons: it obscures the history of legal thinking and it distorts the nature of law. Schmitt adds another discipline to the two he has already addressed and that is philosophy. Whereas the first two chapters were focused on law and sociology; Chapter III includes those two and adds philosophy and theology. Schmitt mentions Hobbes again, but he also includes René Descartes, Gottfried Wilhelm Leibniz, and Jean-Jacques Rousseau. Despite the introduction of theology and philosophy, politics is standing in the background. Hence, Schmitt's Chapter III has the title "Politische Theologie."

As Schmitt had done in the opening sentence of Chapter I, he begins Chapter III with a similarly brief but powerful opening sentence. "All precise concepts of the modern doctrine of the state are secularized theological concepts." ("Alle prägnanten Begriffe der modernen Staatslehre sind säkularisierte theologische Begriffe.") This is self-explanatory with the exception of the term "prägnenten" and that is for two reasons. First, it is unclear what prompted him to choose this term and second, it has a range of meanings. It can mean "exact" but also "terse" and even "pithy." Theological concepts are noted for many things, but precision is typically not one of them. That is because theological terms often refer to things which are transcendent. As Kant had argued in the *Kritik der reinen Vernunft* metaphysical entities are not given to us in "intuitions" they fall outside our faculty of cognition. Perhaps the best ideas that are resistant to precision include God, miracles, and mysticism. As William James argued, mysticism is ineffable and as David Hume maintained, miracles are violations of the laws of nature. Then there is the notion of God, but this is also a question of which God? Is it Zeus, the God of the Greeks? Jehovah, the God of the Jews, the God of the Catholics? Is it the Christ of the Protestants? And this is not even considering the deities of other religions. But such questions do not plague Schmitt because his God is the God of Medieval Catholicism.

Schmitt does not do much to indicate what his deity is; rather, what Schmitt does is to link the "doctrine of the state" ("Staatslehre") to theology in two ways. In the first, he maintains that the state is a secularized notion of the omnipotent God who produced the laws. In the second, he suggests that the hierarchy of the state matches the hierarchy of the Church.[1] It is this parallel structure that holds Schmitt's interest because, like the state, the Church relies on the normal and the usual. But what really concerns Schmitt has been the abnormal and that has been the main focus of *Politische Theologie*. He insists that that focus is found in his earlier books and he lists his *Werte des Staates* (1914), *Politische Romantik* (1919), and *Die Diktatur* (1921) as indications of his concern with the exception.

Sociology does not simply fail in its understanding of law; it misses the crucial point about it. As he had in *Die Diktatur* here he also emphasizes the "state of exception" ("Ausnahmezustand"). In *Die Diktatur* his full focus was on law; here it is on law and theology. There is, he insists, an "analogue significance" ("analoge Bedeutung") between the concept of the "state of exception" in jurisprudence and notion of "miracle" ("Wunder") in theology. Unfortunately, the history of the "state-philosophical idea" ("Staatsphilosophischen Idee") has obscured the connection between jurisprudence and theology. It is Schmitt's intention in his third chapter to recover that connection and to reveal its importance for the concept of sovereignty. He insists that Deism was the beginning of the movement to eliminate the notion of "Wunder" from the world. Deism was a combination of theology and metaphysics, but it seemed to place more importance on the latter. Although Schmitt does not state it, it appears his complaint is not so much about metaphysics itself as it is with the systemization that it represents. It is with the Deists that the "exception" is reduced in importance, but it was the natural law theorists who helped further its exile. Finally, it was the Enlightenment

---

[1] Philosophers, theologians, and Church Historians might take issue with Schmitt's second claim. They would suggest that it was the Church that adopted and adapted the hierarchy of the state and they would suggest that around 300 A.D. the Church realized that it needed to be structurally organized as it grew. Schmitt would have likely been aware of this because of the research by Adolf Harnack, Rudolf Sohm, and Ernst Troeltsch as well as many others. There is no doubt that Sohm disliked the Catholic Church but he was a competent Church historian. Harnack and Troeltsch were more appreciative of Catholic teachings, especially Troeltsch who wrote an exceedingly positive book on Augustine.

("Aufklärung") with its rationalism that completed the elimination of the "case of exception" ("Ausnahmefall") in any form. Schmitt suggests that the theistic convictions of the conservative writers of the counter revolution can be used to support the notion of the personal sovereignty of the monarchs (Schmitt, 1923: 26, 1934: 49, 2015: 43).

The conservative writers of the counter revolution are identified as Bonald, de Maistre, and Donoso Cortés. Schmitt appears to believe that his readers are familiar with each of these three, but these three are probably unknown to many of his twenty-first century readers. Both Louise-Ambroise Visconte de Bonald (1754–1840) and Joseph de Maistre (1753–1821) were French writers who believed that the French Revolution was not just ill-fated but was legally and morally wrong. Juan Donoso Cortés (1809–1853) was a Spanish diplomat who died in Paris and whose convictions matched the other two. All three were conservative Catholic writers—which is why Schmitt appealed to their views. He claims that in their writings one gains the first understanding of a "conceptually clear, systematic analogue" ("begrifflich Klar, systematische Analoge") for the state and society. Schmitt contrasts this favorably with three other types: the mystical, the natural philosophical, and the Romantic. Each of these three are composed of "symbols and pictures" ("Symbole und Bilder") rather than concepts. But it is not with Bonald, or de Maistre that the first clear philosophical analogy between jurisprudence and theology was emphasized. Rather, it was Gottfried Wilhelm Leibniz who first rejected the association between law and medicine and between law and mathematics in favor of the connection between law and theology. Schmitt cites the Latin from *Nova Methodus* § 4 and § 5 but I have not been able to locate the passage that Schmitt cites (Leibniz, 1969: 85–93). What Schmitt cites does not state what he says it does, but Schmitt is probably correct with his claim that Leibniz believed that jurisprudence and theology were similar because they share two principles: the principle of reason and the principle of scripture. But it is unclear how reason would produce a natural theology and a natural jurisprudence. The more plausible connection is something that Leroy Loemker stated in the introductory comments to Leibniz' "Elements of Law" that "The first principles of law and justice are for Leibniz essentially the same as those of his theology, since God is, after all, the supremely powerful lawgiver and the source of all harmony. But the ethical consequences of these metaphysical principles are made clear in law rather than in theology." More importantly, Leibniz does appear to link law with mathematics because he wrote "The doctrine of Right belongs to those sciences which depend on definitions and not on experience and on demonstrations of reason and not of sense; they are problems of law, so to speak, and not of fact" (Leibniz, 1969: 131, 133). Schmitt does not add much to his reference to Leibniz other than to suggest that scripture can produce a book of revelation and order.[2]

Instead, Schmitt returns to his critique of legal positivism and he noted that the Viennese legal scholar Adolf Menzel had indicated that modern sociology had largely taken over the position that natural law had in previous centuries. He does not provide a citation in Menzel's *Naturrecht und Soziologie* (1912) and he offers only a phrase: "political tendencies with the illusion of scholarliness" ("politische Tendenzen mit dem Schein der Wissenschaftlichkeit"). But Schmitt wants to discredit legal positivism much more than the criticism that it is not a to trace legal positivism's final concepts and arguments all the way to the end, one finds only a "deus ex machina." All of the legal positions of executive, police, and others are just variations on theological positions and the "'omnipotence' of the modern law giver" ("'Omnipotenz' des modernen Gesetzgebers") is really nothing more than an "invisible person." He concludes that what is contained in the books is nothing but the language of theology. He adds that in the details the language of law is drawn from theology.[3]

Schmitt insists that most of the charges regarding theology have been polemical because during the "Positivist" age, it was useful to accuse one's opponents of having a legal philosophy that rested upon metaphysical or even theological principles. He suggests that if this accusation is something more than "a mere insult" ("eine bloße Beschimpfung"), then

---

[2] As some one who has spent considerable time studying Leibniz' rationalistic philosophy, Schmitt's comments seem at odds with what Leibniz had written. Schmitt makes no reference to any of Leibniz' principles, such as the Principle of Sufficient Reason, which states that everything that happens has a reason for occurring. We may not be aware of that reason but God has his reason for choosing that to happen. This would seem to go against Schmitt's belief in miracles and especially in "states of exception." See in particular "First Truths" (1680–1684) and "Discourse on Method" (1686). (Leibniz, 1969: 268–269, 303–305).

[3] (Schmitt, 1923: 27–28, 1934: 51, 2015: 44–45). It is a minor point that in the versions from 1923 and 1934, this sentence is included in the paragraph whereas in the 2015 edition it is the beginning of the new paragraph. It is unclear what might have prompted this change.

it goes at least part way to the basis for the inclination toward metaphysics and theology. Historically, one or both were the foundation for the monarchist doctrine of the state and the identification of the King with the theistic God. The question was then of the legitimate basis for this identification. Schmitt freely concedes that there are some jurists who, out of incapability, contradictory argumentation, or out of protest, simply identified the state with God. Schmitt compares this with certain metaphysicians who misuse the name of God for their own purposes.

Hugo Preuß is selected for particular criticism because of his antipathy toward any sort of theology or metaphysics. While Preuß had followed Laband and Jellinek in their elevation of the state, Preuß had intensified the omnipotence of the state and made the state into the highest power—equivalent to God (Schmitt, 1923: 28–29, 1934: 52–53, 2015: 45–46). Schmitt turns to Kelsen who he praises for drawing analogies between law and theology. But he criticizes Kelsen for emphasizing the supposed arbitrariness between the deity and the judge. What Kelsen intended to do was to eliminate this sort of decisionism from law, whereas Schmitt regarded decisionism as the essence of sovereign legal theory. In Schmitt's view, Kelsen intended to follow David Hume and Immanuel Kant in his criticism of the notion of substance. But Schmitt ignores Kelsen's point. Kelsen argued that physics exists as a science without out the need for substance; psychology exists as a science without the need for the soul. So, the "doctrine of law" ("Rechtslehre") can exist without the postulate that the "state" somehow exists. It is a "fiction" as much as the Aristotelian "substance" and the Cartesian "soul" (Descartes, 1985: II 50–60, Kelsen, 2022: 302–304). Instead, Schmitt dismisses the connection between law and physics as irrelevant and insists that the notion of substance is intrinsic to law. He refers to his *Diktatur* where he claimed to have shown this.[4] Schmitt also complains that Kelsen's "confirmation of democracy" ("Bekenntnis zur Demokratie") appears to rest upon the mathematical-natural science manner of thinking. Schmitt claims that it

---

[4] Schmitt provides three pages for reference in *Die Diktatur*—44, 105, and 194. The edition from 1928 is supposedly identical with the first edition of 1921 with the addition of a lengthy appendix (Schmitt, 1928: 213–259). Yet, the pages he gave do not seem to match his claim. Page 44 and its surrounding pages are devoted to the medieval doctrine of ecclesiastical law. Page 105 and those around it focus on central power as found in Montesquieu and others. Page 194 and those preceding and those after are centered on the French revolution of 1830. Schmitt (1928: 90–98, 102–107, and 190–196).

actually shows that Kelsen's political relativism is a metaphysical conception of human understanding that is supposedly free of all miracle and dogma.[5] What this does reveal is that the fundamental understanding of what law is and what it should be is different for what Kelsen contended and what Schmitt believed. Kelsen held that democracy was the closest to the best form of government because it promoted freedom, pluralism, and tolerance. Schmitt was convinced that an authoritarian government was the best because it ensured security, unity, and discipline. Kelsen claimed that his legal philosophy was free from metaphysical ideas; Schmitt argued that that was misleading and readily admitted that his philosophy of law was based upon a metaphysical-theological foundation.

Schmitt begins a new discussion with a new paragraph which opens with some intriguing claims. First, he maintains that it is necessary to clarify the sociological juridical concepts in general before one can set out the sociological concept of sovereignty. Second, he maintains that the sociological juridical concepts are based upon a consequential and radical ideology. Schmitt offers no specific grounds for the former claim and none for the latter. Yet the former might be true but that latter is certainly false. For Kelsen but also for Laband, Anschütz, Preuß, and Weber, ideology was to be avoided because it precluded scholarly thinking. The only thing that would seem to give this credence was Weber's assertion that it is wrong to think that one can have a radical spiritual philosophy of history to counteract the Marxist radical materialistic philosophy of history. But this is to misunderstand both Weber's objections to Rudolf Stammler's Neo-Kantian legal philosophy as well as his comments about not attempting to explain the development of modern capitalism through Protestant principles.[6] Instead, Schmitt launches into a brief discussion of a radical rationalism of the Marxists conjoined with the radical economic theory to develop the radical materialistic philosophy of history. But Schmitt suggested that it was easy for that to transform

---

[5] Schmitt does not cite the title of this work but indicated that it appeared in 1920 in the *Archiv für Sozialwissenschaft und Sozialpolitik*. However, no such publication is listed in Thomas Olechowski's bibliography in his biography of Hans Kelsen, at least not with the page number that Schmitt gave (84) (Olechowski, 2020: 935). Schmitt may have referred to an early version of "Wesen und Werte der Demokratie" but the page numbers do coincide with the version that Schmitt gave.

[6] It would take at least one if not two essays to explain how radically wrong Schmitt is in his assertion. It is not really necessary here because Schmitt immediately changes the subject.

into the radical irrational anarcho-syndicalist socialism (Schmitt, 1923: 30, 1934: 55–56, 2015: 48). Schmitt insists that the problem is when one side seeks to explain everything by reducing it to one's own side. He gives two examples: (1) when the materialists seek to explain phenomena without recourse to any non-material causes and (2) when the spiritualist rejects any and all material factors in seeking to understand some particular phenomenon. Schmitt insists that this leads not to any explication but to a caricature of an explanation. Schmitt uses Engel's claim that the Calvinist doctrine of predestination is an illustration of the senselessness and unpredictability of the capitalist competitive struggles. Schmitt allows that sociological terms and theories have their places and their uses, but he does question sociological methods. He insists that certain sociological methods will deliver certain sociological results but that these are predicated on certain questionable assumptions. He makes reference to Max Weber who, according to Schmitt, insisted that one's vocation determined how one considered legal matters and Schmitt pointed to the ways in which judges, administrators, and officials evaluate evidence and pronounce verdicts. Schmitt admits that this is not yet a sociological concept of law because it has elements of psychology in it. It is still a question of psychological motivation. This is a sociological problem as well, but he insisted it was not a sociology of a concept. Schmitt again draws attention to the ways in which jurists and professors are certain types of people. He points to two different groups of individuals. The first were found in Hegelian philosophical circles and those budding professors viewed social and economic conditions through the contemplative lens of "absolute consciousness." The second group are the contemporary Kelsen theorists who consider that bureaucrats tend to function in accordance with their concepts of political power. Both are sociological types and both provide "portraits." But Schmitt criticizes them for being similar to those provided in beautiful literature.

Schmitt's intention appears to be to differentiate between those literary portraits and his scholarly rigor. In the paragraph that follows his earlier discussion of the Hegelian and Kelsenian ideologies, he uses some form of the word "concept" ("Begriff") fourteen times. But this paragraph is among the least clear in all of *Politische Theologie*. He writes about structure and substance, but it is not clear what he means. When he writes about things being radical, it is not obvious why he is convinced they are. Two examples should suffice: "the last, radical systematic structure" ("die letzte, radikal systematischer Struktur") and "the ideal of the radical conceptuality" ("das Ideel der radikalen Begrifflichkeit"). What he seems to be attempting to distinguish is between "sociological reality" and "social reality" where the former is simply a construct and the latter reflects reality. One is simply a manner of thinking while the other captures what has actually happened. This supposition gains support when Schmitt refers to the notion of sovereignty in the seventeenth century. Schmitt referred to the idea that there were two spiritual substances and that the monarchy "'mirrored'" ("'spiegelte'") the Cartesian concept of God. Rather than dismissing this as an unwanted intrusion of metaphysics into reality, Schmitt suggests that it was a means of reflecting the historical-political reality. In fact, he insists that the metaphysical picture is the actual reflection of the form of the political organization and it is his intent to show that that still applies. This is the identity of the sociology of the concept of sovereignty. He refers to Edward Caird who, in his book on Auguste Comte, said that "Metaphysics is the most intensive and clearest expression of an epoch." ("Metaphysik der intensivste und klarste Ausdruck einer Epoche ist.") (Schmitt, 1923: 31–32, 1934: 59–60, 2015: 50–51).

The imitation of the immutable decrees of the divinity was, according to Schmitt, the ideal of the state legal existence according to the Rationalists of the eighteenth century. Schmitt referred to a number of French thinkers but his view was best expressed by a quotation by a scholar writing on Rousseau. Schmitt quotes two sentences: the first indicated that the state was just a continuation of God's creation, but the second is explicit: "The prince is the Cartesian God transposed into the political world." ("Le prince est le Dieu cartésien transpose dans le monde politique.") For Schmitt, this is the identification of the king with God. This is the complete identification between the metaphysical, political, and sociological representation of the sovereign and reveals the sovereign as the original creator of laws and the regulator of the state judiciary. Schmitt suggested that Descartes had contemplated the deity who constructed the world was analogous to the builder who constructs a house. Schmitt moves from Descartes to Hobbes and insists that despite Hobbes' nominalism and his natural science-founded philosophy believed that the state was the Leviathan. For Schmitt, this was no form of anthropomorphism but was a "methodological and systematic necessity of his juridical thought" ("methodologische und systematische Notwendigkeit seines juristischen Denkens") (Schmitt, 1923: 33, 1934: 61, 2015: 52). But Schmitt pointed out that the comparison between the architect and the world creator still contained the "unclarity of the concept of causality" ("Unklarheit des Kausalitätsbegriffs"). The world creator was both the originator and the law giver—and was the legitimate authority. But for the Enlightenment until the French Revolution this role had been assigned to the legislature.

Schmitt observed that throughout much of that period, the natural sciences exerted particularly strong influence on political thought and judicial thinking. The influence was shown by the manner in which legal thinking mirrored the natural sciences in that it reflected the general validity of both. Just as there are no exceptions to the laws of physics, there are no exceptions to legal laws. Schmitt draws specific attention to the Deist "world picture" ("Weltbild") in which the sovereign is located outside of the world and is regarded as the maker of the world as a machine. Once made, the creator is not needed—"The machine runs now by itself." ("Die Machine läufte jetzt von selbst.") He also emphasized that the Deist God does not will particulars; but wills only the general. This notion, which was shared by Leibniz and Malebranche, was adapted by Rousseau with his "volonte Générale." But here the "general will" is regarded as the sovereign will of the people. Yet Rousseau's "general will" shares the same generality found in the deity of Leibniz. What is lost in these conceptions is the personal element and the power of decisions. The new conceptions also carry the conviction that by definition the will of the people is as beneficial as God's will was considered to be. The laws of the people are supreme just as God's commandments are supreme. But Schmitt insists that the necessity which gives rise to the correctness of the people is different than the correctness of a sovereign. To bolster his claim, Schmitt insisted that the absolute monarch needed to intervene between two competing groups with their own particular interests, and he made his decision alone and thereby founded the state's unity. He clarified that this was not really a decisionist move, but it represents the natural and organic unity of his people. In this sense, the monarch cannot represent the Deist God. In Schmitt's understanding, the Theist and the Deist concept of God is not understandable in the "political metaphysics." This claim is not to be taken for the complete end of Deist thinking. Rather, its aftereffects continued to linger for a considerable time. Schmitt then makes a number of highly questionable claims. First, he insists that the "reasonable-pragmatic faith" ("vernünftig-pragmatischer Glaube") took the "voice of the people" to be the "voice of God" and that it was the basis for Thomas Jefferson's election as president. But this is a misreading of both the American electorate of the era as well as the 1800 election. It is also a misreading of the congressional voting of 1801 which saw Jefferson confirmed as president. Second, Schmitt misreads Tocqueville's description of the power of religion in America. In addition, Tocqueville was describing an America that had already changed substantially since Jefferson was inaugurated. The fact that Tocqueville could travel as far West as he did was partially because of Jefferson's Louisiana Purchase. Americans of the era did not believe that the state's love swept over the citizens' life just as God did over the world. Nor did the Americans believe that the state is the alpha and omega of all things, just as God created everything and everything returned to God. The state was certainly not an Aristotelian First and Final Cause. Schmitt does not explain his justifications for his claims, but suddenly moves to discuss Kelsen again. He contends that Kelsen's democracy is an expression of his relativistic, impersonal science. Schmitt concludes this paragraph with the observation that Kelsen's legal philosophy was an outgrowth of the political theology and metaphysics of the nineteenth century (Schmitt, 1923: 33–34, 1934: 62–63, 2015: 51–53).

Much of the commentary on Chapter III has been highly critical. But the final two pages of Schmitt's Chapter III reveal him at his finest. He is able to distill several centuries of philosophical and theological thought into two paragraphs and he does so with clarity and verve. He begins by indicating that the concept of God in the seventeenth and eighteenth centuries was a transcendent deity and that the notion of the monarch was also considered over and above the people. But this concept of a transcendent God was being replaced by the notion of an immanent deity. As a result, the rule of the state also lost its transcendence and became part of the world. Schmitt lays out the identities: the identity of the ruler with the rules; the organic theory of the state with the identity of the state and sovereignty. There is also Krabbe's "rechtsstaatsliche" doctrine of sovereignty and legal order; and finally, Kelsen's doctrine of the state with the legal order. In each of these transformations, the substance is minimized until it mostly disappears. It was only with the writers of the Restoration Era that there were efforts to push back against this process. It was with those writers that the notion of "political theology" was invented, and it was with them that the struggle to fight against this anti-God and anti-theology movement began to take shape. Instead of discussing this, Schmitt lays out how the "anti-God" movement progressed. He observed that it was August Comte who had identified Proudhon who was likely the instigator of the struggle against God and he noted that Bakunin carried it on. This should not be taken to mean that there was one single motivated force that was behind the struggle against God. Schmitt suggests that this struggle was motivated by a number of different political and sociological factors. These included the antipathy against the conservative adherence to churchly Christianity. It included the interconnected throne and alter. It also included the literary movement to rid literature of any centrality of religion. Finally, it was the impulse to place bourgeoise order on the citizens themselves. But Schmitt admits that none of these "causes" have yet to be investigated and clarified. He also allows that even the philosophical movements have not been adequately addressed. He does insist that there is a clear line from the philosophical ideas to the acceptance by the masses in respect to this movement to eliminate God from the world. Schmitt places much of the blame on Hegel with his pantheism and how that was adapted by the Right-wing Hegelians. But it was the Left-wing followers of Hegel that won the day. They were the ones who replaced the concept of God with the notion of humanity. To most of the masses, it did not matter whether the replacement of God with humanity was based upon a Hegelian imminence pantheism or a positivistic equality, the result was still the same. It was a rejection of metaphysics and with that theology. This was nothing but atheism and was promoted by the Left-Hegelians. Here, Schmitt's lineage is not so clear: he suggests that neither Proudhon nor the young Marx and Engels really pushed an anarchist position. What the young Engels did note was "The essence of the state as the religion is the angst that humanity has of itself." ("Das Wesen des Staates wie der Religion ist die Angst der Menschheit vor sich selber.").

There are, Schmitt declares, two major themes to be drawn from his brief historical overview. First is the setting aside of all theistic and transcendent representations. Second, is the construction of a new concept of legitimacy. This new concept of legitimacy has lost all possible evidence. In this onslaught nothing appeared to be able to stand in its way: neither the private law's patrimonial position of the period of the Restoration, nor the piety's attachment to this feeling. Instead, the Revolution of 1848 eliminated all of the transcendent elements and replaced them with positivism. This meant a rearrangement of the notion of law; it became a mere question of power—the supposed power of the "People." In simple terms this meant that the democratic concept of legitimacy to the place of the monarchial one. Donoso Cortés recognized that the monarchial period had ended and that there was no more royalty because there was no longer a king. There was also no longer the notion of legitimacy in the traditional sense. The sole consequence is a dictator with his notion of authority. Schmitt cites Hobbes: "Authority, not truth make law." ("Autoritas, non veritas facit legem.") There is no longer the legitimate ruler; only the one who holds power. Truth no longer matters; only force. This is the conclusion that Hobbes was compelled to reach, even if he had combined his "mathematical relativism" with the consequences of his "decisionist thinking."

Schmitt concludes Chapter III and the end of his 1923 essay with some final comments. He maintains that an extensive exploration of decisionism and a proper evaluation of Donoso Cortés do not yet exist. He does not intend to provide it here but he does intend to draw some attention to the fact that Donoso Cortés' juridical philosophy now rested upon Medieval theology. Schmitt insists that all of Donoso Cortés' perceptions, as well as all of his arguments are, to the "last atom," founded upon this theology. It is as if Donoso Cortés ignored all of the newly created mathematical principles and ignored each of the recently discovered laws of natural science and instead embraced the decisionism and the personal decisions in his thinking (Schmitt, 1923: 35, 1934: 66, 2015: 55).

Schmitt's Chapter III is far more wide-ranging and less structured than the previous two chapters. It is more philosophical and theological than it is legal. He is less likely to provide references or even hints for his sources. While he was content to provide the benefits of scholarly apparatus in Chapters I and II, here he apparently has no inclination to do so. The fact that he ends with a comment about Donoso Cortés and does not provide a conclusion to his essay serves to underscore the subtitle of *Four Chapters*. It is not until Chapter IV that the reader gets a sense of Schmitt's ultimate conclusion concerning the concept of sovereignty.

REFERENCES

Descartes, R. (1985). *The Philosophical Writings of Descartes* (Volumes I and II). (John Cottingham, Robert Stoothoff, Dugald Murdoch, Trans.). Cambridge University Press.

Kelsen, H. (2022). *Veröffentlichte Schriften 1921–1923*. Herausgegeben von Matthias Jestaedt In Kooperation mit dem Hans Kelsen-Institut. Mohr Siebeck. *Hans Kelsen Werke*. Band 7.

Kelsen, H. (2013). *Veröffentlichte Schriften 1918–1920*. Herausgegeben von Matthias Jestaedt In Kooperation mit dem Hans Kelsen-Institut. Mohr Siebeck. *Hans Kelsen Werke*. Band 4.

Leibniz, G. W. (1969). *Philosophical Papers and Letters*. (Leroy E. Loemker, Eds.). D. Reidel Publishing Company.

Olechowski, T. (2020). *Hans Kelsen. Biographie eines Rechtswissenschaftlers*. Mohr Siebeck.

Schmitt, C. (2015). *Politische Theologie. Vier Kapitel zur Lehre von der Souveränität*. Duncker & Humblot. Zehnte Auflage.

Schmitt, C. (1934). *Politische Theologie. Vier Kapitel zur Lehre von der Souveränität*. Duncker & Humblot.

Schmitt, C. (1928). *Die Diktatur. Von den Anfängen des modernen Souveränitäts-gedanken bis zum proletarischen Klassenkampf. Zweite Auflage, mit einem Anhang: Die Diktatur des Reichspräsidenten nach Art. 48 der Weimarer Verfassung*. Verlag von Duncker & Humblot.

Schmitt, C. (1923). Soziologie des Souveränitätsbegriffes und politische Theologie. In *Hauptprobleme der Soziologie. Erinnerungsgabe für Max Weber* (pp. 3–36). Herausgegeben von Melchior Palyi. Duncker & Humblot. II. Band.

CHAPTER 6

The Counter Revolution and Decisionism

Abstract Carl Schmitt's Chapter IV differs from the previous in at least two substantial ways. First, it has little to do with sovereignty and almost nothing to do with sociology. That may be why Schmitt chose not to include it in the version found in the volume in honor of Max Weber. Second, while Chapter IV does discuss the importance of decisions, that concept is frequently obscured by Schmitt's discussions of some counter-revolutionaries, his insistence on the need for a dictator, and the modern emphasis on economics. The chapter is about the philosophy of the state as embodied in the thinking of the counter revolution ("Zur Staatsphilosophie der Gegenrevolution"). Donoso Cortés is mentioned in the subtitle as are De Maistre and Bonald. Schmitt denounces democracy because it leads to eternal discussions and he praises authoritarianism because its leaders are decisive. Decisions, not discussions can be regarded as the theme of this chapter. Unlike the previous three chapters, Chapter IV does not have many connections to the others and can be read as a self-standing essay.

Keywords Counter-revolutionaries · Decisionism · De Maistre · Bonald · Authority

Carl Schmitt's final chapter (Chapter IV) differs from the previous three chapters in at least two substantial ways. First, it has little to do with sovereignty and almost nothing to do with sociology. That may be why Schmitt chose not to include it in the version found in the volume in honor of Max Weber. Second, while Chapter IV does discuss the importance of decisions, that concept is frequently obscured by Schmitt's discussions of some counter-revolutionaries, his insistence on the need for a dictator, and the modern emphasis on economics. These two reasons account for the slightly truncated discussion of Chapter IV.

The title of Chapter IV ("Zur Staatsphilosophie der Gegenrevolution") indicates it is about the philosophy of the state as embodied in the thinking of the counter revolution. Donoso Cortés is mentioned in the subtitle as are de Maistre and Bonald. Schmitt denounces democracy because it leads to eternal discussions and he praises authoritarianism because its leaders are decisive. Decisions, not discussions can be regarded as the theme of this chapter. Unlike Chapters I, II, and III, Chapter IV does not have many connections to the others and can be read as a self-standing essay. While Schmitt makes a number of important points and much of what he writes is provocative, it does not appear persuasive—in part because it ends on a highly questionable political note.

Schmitt's opening sentence of his final chapter may not be as shocking as the sentence that began Chapter I, but it is still startling. It is startling for two reasons: first, it does not begin with any comment on state government, but on the German Romantics. Second, it does not mention any of the three counter-revolutionary writers but complains about "eternal discussion" ("ewige Gespräch"). The first half of the sentence contains what is notable; the second half seems almost an afterthought. "For the German Romantics, there is one specific characteristic: eternal discussion." ("Den deutschen Romantikern ist eine originelle Vorstellung eigentümlich: das ewige Gespräch.") Schmitt suggests that that sums up the Romantic's spirit. In contrast, de Maistre, Bonald, and Donoso Cortés had regarded "eternal discussion" as "a fantasy product from a terrible comedian" ("ein Phantasie-produkt von grausiger Komik"). During the period between the Revolution of 1789 and the Revolution of 1848, the counter-revolutionary thinkers countered the "eternal discussion" with the emphasis on decisions. In fact, it became the central theme of their political thinking. Instead of one group of people finding common ground with another group of people, Catholic doctrinaires insisted on clear oppositions. Schmitt quoted Cardinal Newman's dictum that there is no medium between "catholicity and atheism." This is the sharpness of an "either-or" and Schmitt suggested that this is preferable to listening to an "eternal discussion" even if this sharpness sounds like a dictatorship (Schmitt, 1934: 69, 2015: 59).

Schmitt turns to the notions of tradition and typicality and he contrasts its slow and steady movement of the Restoration with the "activist spirit" of the Revolution. Given Schmitt's insistence on decisiveness, this praise for tradition seems odd. But it should be regarded as a careful approach as opposed to the carelessness of the revolutionary. He defends tradition against the charge that it is completely irrational and totally sentimental. He also contrasted Bonald's notion of traditionalism with that of de Maistre and of Donoso. Bonald's notion has a far different structure than either of theirs, which leads Schmitt to observe that Bonald's reveals itself as surprisingly German. Yet he also indicates that Bonald's faith in tradition differs from that found in Schelling's philosophy of nature, Adam Müller's mixture of oppositions, or in Hegel's faith in history. Instead, tradition is the single path to winning back faith in metaphysics. Bonald believed that the understanding of the individual is too weak and too poor for him to recognize the truth. In contrast to those three Germans, Bonald contended that to use history to try to understand the truth is like a blindman leading a herd of blind people. Schelling's traditional faith in nature, Müller's traditional faith in oppositions, and Hegel's supposed faith in the dialectical negations of history are faulty. Instead of these complicated philosophical approaches, what really matters are the pure oppositions: good and evil, God and the devil, and between life and death. These are "either-or"; what they are not are syntheses or some "higher third" ("'höheres Drittes'").

Schmitt turns from Bonald to de Maistre and he stresses de Maistre's special preference for sovereignty, which Schmitt says is essentially the notion of decision. De Maistre argued that the value of the state was that it makes decisions, and Schmitt noted that this was similar to de Maistre's claim that the value of the Church rested in its power of decision. But the Church is superior because its decisions are never wrong: the Pope is infallible. Schmitt suggests that the monarch has a power that approaches that of the Pope and that the king's decision is also absolute. De Maistre maintained that there was a clear opposition between all anarchists and all monarchists. The anarchists all subscribe to the same axiom: "The people are good and the magistrate corruptible." ("le people est bon et le magistrat corruptible.") (Schmitt, 1934: 70–71, 2015: 60). De

Maistre declared the opposite and that the authority was good as such because the government is stable. It is stable mostly because it possesses the power to decide, and to decide without delay and without appeal. It is essentially above reproach and cannot be reevaluated.

The next theme is the revolutionary radicalism of the proletarian Revolution of 1848 which was infinitely deeper and far more consequential than that of peasant revolt of 1789. In a similar manner, the intensity of the importance of decision also grew for the counter-revolutionary legal theorists of the state. It is only by recognizing this that one can understand the development of ideas from de Maistre to Donoso Cortés. This was the development from the concept of legitimacy to the notion of dictatorship. Schmitt insists that all political ideas are based upon the nature of humans. Either humans are by nature good or by nature evil. Any attempt to go avoid this question with references to educational systems or economic explanations is subject to fail. The question whether humans are naturally good or naturally bad is fundamental. Schmitt spends some time discussing how the Rationalists believed that human beings were naturally good but that they were fundamentally stupid and primitive. They needed to be educated. Rousseau insisted on the power of education to change human nature and Fichte maintained that it was necessary to forcibly educate the masses. But this belief changed with Marxism because the Marxists thought the notion of the nature of human beings to be superfluous. It was superfluous because humans were affected only by economic and social conditions. Marxists contended that if one changes these conditions then one can change human nature. Any question about the natural goodness or natural evilness is merely a residue of theological ideas and is a derivative of the authority, state, and government. The remainder of this paragraph is a confusing mixture of theology and psychiatry. Schmitt contrasts the Catholic doctrine of original sin with the Lutheran notion of forgiveness. But he then again brings up Proudhon's atheistic anarchism, and while Proudhon appeared to have agreed with Luther, his estimation of authority is closer to that of the Grand Inquisitor.

The following paragraph is not much clearer. There are references to Nietzsche's "Will to Power" ("Wille zur Macht") and references to modern psychiatry. But the main focus appears to be a continuation of Schmitt's comments on whether human beings are naturally good or naturally evil. It appears that Schmitt endorses Donoso Cortés' extremely negative assessment of humankind. Schmitt refers to his contention that humans are no better than the reptiles that he stamps upon. He suggests that humans blindly struggle in a labyrinth and that they are sailing on a ship with no destination or purpose. Schmitt concludes this paragraph with a declaration of the current "bloody decision battle" ("blutige Entscheidungsschlacht") between Catholicism and atheistic socialism (Schmitt, 1934: 74–75, 2015: 63).

Schmitt turns to Donoso's criticisms of liberalism. Liberals do not want to decide which side to take in this battle between Catholics and socialists; instead, they want to discuss the matter, thereby postponing the need to make a decision. Rather than acting, liberals want to discuss this in the press and in parliament. But, people recognize this uncertainty and they understand that parliament does not want to act but to paralyze the king so that he cannot act. Schmitt insists that liberals want a God, but one who is not active. Similarly, they want a king, but one who has no power. Liberals promote the ideals of freedom and equality, but not for the under classes. They believe that education and property render them superior. They have displaced the aristocracy of blood and family and replaced it with the "shameful domination of money aristocracy" ("unverschämte Herrschaft der Geldaristokratie"). In Schmitt's opinion, this is the stupidest and most ordinary form of aristocracy. Liberals do not want the sovereignty of the king nor the sovereignty of the people. Since liberals reject the sovereignty of the king and the sovereignty of the people, Schmitt then asks: "What then do they really want?" ("Was will sie also eigentlich?") (Schmitt, 1934: 75–76, 2015: 64).

These contradictions in liberalism have been noticed not only by reactionaries such as Donoso and Stahl; they have also been noticed by revolutionaries such as Marx and Engels. These contradictions in liberalism have also been remarked upon by people in the middle. Schmitt invokes Lorenz von Stein who insisted that French liberals wanted a particular type pf monarch. A king who was simply the administrator who stood above the parties; and one who would carry out the people's will. But the French liberals also did not trust the king as a person and they did not trust him to carry out the people's will. Schmitt quotes von Stein: "'No human acuity', said Stein, 'is sharp enough to conceptually solve this opposition.'" ("'Kein menschlicher Scharfsinn,' sagt Stein, 'ist scharf genug, um diesen Gegensatz begrifflich zu lösen.'") (Schmitt, 1934: 76–77, 2015: 64–65). Schmitt concludes that this must seem doubly remarkable to the liberals who believe that they are the party of rationalism.

Schmitt refers to F.J. Stahl, the Prussian conservative, who had a simple explanation. The hate against royalty and aristocracy drives the liberals to the left. But the angst for the radical democrats and socialist who will take away their property drives them back again to the right. They believe that the Right's strong military will protect them. Yet Schmitt believes that the liberal regard both sides as enemies, and "so he swings between both of his enemies and would like to deceive them both" ("so schwankt er zwischen seinen beiden Feinden und möchte beide betrügen"). Lorenz von Stein had an entirely different explanation: oppositions and contradictions are just a part of life. It is the essence of life to have ever new oppositions and to slowly create a new harmony. That Schmitt thinks this is ridiculous is indicated by his "etc. etc." ("usw. usw."). It is also indicated by his claim that "Such 'organic' thinking" ("Solchen 'organischen' Denkens") would not appear possible to de Maistre or Donoso Cortés. Schmitt reminds his readers that both de Maistre and Donoso Cortés were diplomats so they understood the need for compromises. He immediately adds "However, the systematic and metaphysical compromise would be unfathomable to them." ("Aber der systematische und metaphysische Kompromiß war ihnen unfaßbar.") (Schmitt, 1934: 78, 2015: 65–66). It is unfathomable to decide to suspend the decision at the decisive moment. It is unfathomable to deny what absolutely must be decided. It is unfathomable because this can only be some peculiar pantheist insanity. Schmitt suggests that to Cortés this appeared to be a crazy interim response to the question Christ or Barrabas—a response that appears to be either a "motion to recess or an invitation for an investigative commission" ("Vertagungsantrag oder der Einsetzung einer Untersuchungskommission"). Schmitt insisted that this approach was not an accident but rather was grounded in liberal metaphysics. He insisted that the bourgeoise is the class of freedom of speech and freedom of press. This did not arise out of some psychological or economical condition. Instead, the idea of liberal right of freedom came directly out of North America. Schmitt refers to Georg Jellinek who had argued that human rights grew out of the Protestant insistence on tolerance. Schmitt does not provide a reference but Jellinek had published "The Explanation of Human- and Citizen Rights" ("Die Erklärung der Menschen- und Bürgerrechte"). There Jellinek had argued that human rights were not a result of French revolutionary thinking; but rather, were founded upon early

New England religious principles.[1] Schmitt suggests that Protestantism is responsible for the grounding of this ridiculous notion of human rights and that the Catholics are right to criticize it or even to reject it. As he had already dismissed the economic dominance, Schmitt contends that the American economic postulate of free trade and unrestricted competition are also based upon the liberal metaphysical foundation. His explicit critique is that these economic ideas are faulty, but his implicit complaint is that liberals are hypocritical in the denunciation of the metaphysical (and theological) principles which under lie Catholic anti-liberalism when the liberals have their own metaphysical (and theological) principles. Principles which they basically deny having. Schmitt praises Donoso Cortés for focusing his radical spirituality only on the "theology of the opponents" ("Theologie des Gegners"). Schmitt also commends him for not theologizing himself. Schmitt insists that Donoso Cortés never indulges in mystical combinations and refrains from offering up some orphic oracle. Instead, Donoso Cortés' letters on the actual political situation were always sober and his conclusions were often gruesome in absence of illusions. Donoso Cortés was Spanish but he had no "hint of Don Quixote." Instead, his insights were often penetrating and even "striking" ("Frappant"). Schmitt offers two examples: first, Donoso's definition of the bourgeois as the "'Clasa discutidora'" or the ("'discussing class'"). Second, knowing that religion is at the basis for free speech and freedom of the press. Schmitt allows that this may not be the last word on liberalism, but he insists that there is an amazing gap in Continental liberalism. Schmitt is amazed, if not appalled, by what Condorcet and even Wolzendorff have as an ideal of political life. Not only do the legislators engage in continuous discussion but that the entire population is expected to debate. In Schmitt's opinion, this changes the "human society" ("menschliche Gesellschaft") into a "monstrous club" ("ungeheuren Klub") (Schmitt, 1934: 79–80, 2015: 66–67). Schmitt contended that Donoso believed that this was the method that liberals used to avoid having to take responsibility and why they emphasized freedom of speech and freedom of the press. This was the means to postpone the need to make any decision. By discussing each political instance, liberalism seeks to dissolve "the metaphysical truth" ("die metaphysiche Wahrheit") in discussion. Its essence is handling of half-truths and it hopes to postpone the definitive

---

[1] Jellinek's work is found in Schnur (1964: 1–77). The relevant pages include.36–38 and 47–54.

conflict; the "bloody battle of decision" ("blutige Entscheidungsschlact") and to transform it into a parliamentarian debate. By doing so, liberalism hopes to eternally suspend decisions through "eternal discussion." Schmitt begins the next paragraph with another one of his provocative sentences.

"Dictatorship is the opposite of discussion." ("Diktatur ist der Gegensatz zur Diskussion.") Schmitt insists that for Donoso Cortés decisionism was the spiritual art of the extreme case. That is why Donoso Cortés could despise the liberals and respect the anarchistic-atheist socialists. Donoso could never respect the "middling" liberals but he did respect the diabolic greatness of his deadly enemy. Schmitt writes: "In Proudhon, he [Donoso] believed to see a demon." ("In Proudhon, glaubt er einen Dämon zu sehen.") During that time, satanism was not regarded as some sort of paradox but was considered "a strong, intellectual principle" ("ein starkes, intellektuelles Prinzip"). In order to create paradise on earth, God must be banished. This meant that the roles of God and devil needed to be reversed. Schmitt adds that the later anarchists regarded Proudhon as a "moralizing petty bourgeoise" ("moralisierender kleinbürger") who had the authority of the father of the family and who held fast to the "principle of the monogamous family" ("monogamen Familienprinzip") (Schmitt, 1934: 80–81, 2015: 67).

It was Bakunin who drew the consequences of absolute naturalism and that meant a fight against theology. It also implied the expansion of Satan because Satan was naturally against the supernatural deity. Bakunin had the correct form for his correct thinking and that meant repudiating the dualism of Christianity. There is nothing natural about good or evil; these are theological constructs just like the theological doctrine of God and sin. These are manifestations of power and dominance. Morality leads back to theology. Every manifestation of authority is power, so the fatherly authority is nothing more than power. Thus, the principle of the monogamous family is nothing but a means of domination and a return to the supposed matriarchal paradise. Donoso recognized this for what it was; the attempt to link all morality to theology and then all morality to the political. Then the final stage is to eliminate all decisions in favor of a "paradisical here and now" ("paradiesischen Diesseits") with its natural life and problem-less body (Schmitt, 1934: 81–82, 2015: 68).

"Today there is nothing more modern than the fight against politics." ("Heute ist nichts moderner als der Kampf gegen das Politische.")

Thus begins Schmitt's complaint about modern society which sees everything in terms of economics. It does not matter who it is, all believe in economics to the detriment of the political. Schmitt provides an illustrative and almost exhaustive list: from the American finance people, to the industrial technicians, to the Marxist socialists, to the anarcho-syndicalist revolutionaries—they all think in terms of economic factors and not in political ideas. There are no political problems; only organizational-technical issues and social-economic tasks. In their view, the unserious domination of politics has been replaced by the seriousness of economic life. In today's dominating manner of economic thought, a political idea is no longer relevant. As Max Weber had suggested, the modern state has in reality become a giant business. Every political thought has been eliminated in favor of economic interest. All political disputes have been rejected in favor of technical discussions. Or, they simply disappear into "eternal talk." Regardless which side, the core of the political idea, its demanding moralistic decision is gone. In contrast, the actual significance of the counter-revolutionary philosophy of the state is predicated on consequence of the decision. Indeed, the increase in the strength of the notion of decision has supplanted the concept of legitimacy. Schmitt claims that when Donoso Cortés recognized that the time of the monarchy had passed because there was no longer a king and no one had the courage to be one, that it was the time for decisionism. This led to the concept of the dictatorship. De Maistre had already reduced the state to the moment of decision. That meant no justifications and no discussions, "thus simply out of nothing is the absolute decision created" ("also aus dem Nichts geschaffene absolute Entscheidung").

Schmitt concludes that for Donoso, any talk about legitimacy was nothing but words. Only a dictator could fight such radical evil. But Schmitt adds that the anarchist is also a decisive individual and that each side of the battle between authority and anarchy is absolutely certain that his side is right. This is a clear antithesis: de Maistre says that every government is necessarily absolute and the anarchist would agree. The difference is that the anarchist believes that humans are good and regimes are corrupt; therefore, it is necessary to fight against the government as all governments are dictatorships. In Schmitt's opinion, the anarchist is as much a decisionist as the deciding dictator. Schmitt concludes his final chapter with the observation that Bakunin, who was the greatest anarchist of the nineteenth century, regarded himself as the theoretical theologian

of the anti-theological; but that meant in practice that he was the dictator
of the anti-dictatorship (Schmitt, 1934: 83–84, 2015: 69–70).

CONCLUDING COMMENTS

This chapter may seem as satisfactory as the first three were because
it lacks the cohesiveness and focus of Chapters I, II, and III. While
those chapters are sometimes lacking in specific references, this chapter
has almost totally dispensed with scholarly citations. These points reveal
Chapter IV's shortcomings but that does not imply that it lacks scholarly
value. Schmitt's political leanings are more pronounced and his claims
stronger than in the earlier chapters. Chapter I had "The Sovereign is
he who decides about the state of exception." And Chapter III had "All
precise concepts of the modern doctrine of state are secularized theological concepts."[2] Just as Chapter I and Chapter III had their own
compelling sentences; Chapter IV has its own: "Diktatur ist der Gegensatz zu Diskussion"—"Dictatorship is the opposite of discussion." The
difference is that the first two were the opening sentence of those chapters, whereas this one is found in the second page before the end of
Chapter IV. Schmitt had begun Chapter IV with his complaint about
"eternal discussions" and he moves to conclude both the chapter and
Politische Theologie with an emphasis on decisions. "The sovereign is the
one who decides the case of exception" is amended here to the dictator
is "the one who decides everything." Schmitt has belied his insistence
that it is the exceptional case that is important; instead, it is simply the
matter of decision for each and every case. In Schmitt's opinion, discussion is not just bothersome; it is pernicious. That is why dictatorship
is the opposite of discussion. But this has far-reaching implications and
repercussions. This implies that there is no need for the dictator to seek
counsel and no requirement for expert opinion; it is merely a matter of
decision. That decision may be good or bad and for Schmitt the outcome
of the decision is immaterial. Instead, it is only the act of deciding that
has worth. But without adequate information, the dictator's decision is
arbitrary. Schmitt's contention that the dictator and the deity are both

---

[2] The opening sentence in Chapter I is "Souverän ist, wer über den Ausnahmezustand
entscheidet" and the opening sentence of Chapter III is "All prägneten Begriffe der
modernen Staatslehre sind säkularisierte theologische Begriffe" (Schmitt, 1934: 11, 49,
80, 2015: 13, 43, 67).

sovereigns is undermined by whether one believes in Leibniz' rationalist God or the theologian's God of mercy, that deity does not decide things simply according to his will. He is either motivated to decide based upon knowing the past, present, and the future. Or he is prompted to decide based upon complete goodness and beneficence. But Schmitt's dictator has given up the "theology" half of *Politische Theologie* for the first half of "politics." But even here, the politician is expected to have an informed opinion for his or her own decisions. Schmitt's dictator goes beyond even Hobbes' Leviathan—Schmitt's dictator is pure will. But Schmitt's sovereign lacks all traces of sovereignty; there is only unbridled power. It is hard to believe that Carl Schmitt would think that a person without constraints would be a good leader; but in his "Der Führer schütz das Recht" Schmitt placed his unconditional faith in Hitler's power and he contended that only Hitler could save Germany from repeating its past mistakes.[3] In Schmitt's opinion, Hitler did not "stand under justice"; rather Hitler himself was the highest justice. It is Hitler who would distinguish between "friend and foe" (Schmitt, 1988: 200, 203). The dictatorship is the opposite of discussion; since the errors of Weimar were the result of endless discussions, the Third Reich would not suffer the same mistakes. It is probably not a coincidence that Schmitt wrote "Der Führer schütz das Recht" in 1934; the same year that he chose to republish *Politische Theologie*.

References

Schmitt, C. (2015). *Politische Theologie. Vier Kapitel zur Lehre von der Souveränität*. Duncker & Humblot. Zehnte Auflage.

Schmitt, C. (1988). *Positionen und Begriffe. im Kampf mit Weimar-Genf-Versailles 1923–1939*. Duncker & Humblot.

Schmitt, C. (1934). *Politische Theologie. Vier Kapital zur Lehre von der Souveränitat*. Duncker & Humblot.

Schnur, R. Hrsg. (1964). *Zur Geschichte der Erklärung der Menschenrechte*. Wissenschaftliche Buchgesellschaft.

[3] "Der Führer schütz das Recht" is found in *Positionen und Begriffe* which was first published in 1940. The edition from 1988 is an unchanged version from the first edition.

CHAPTER 7

Political Theology and Sovereignty Today

Abstract This chapter is more than just a summary or a conclusion; it considers Schmitt's concept of sovereignty and his notion of "political theology. This concluding chapter has three parts. The first concerns the continual interest in the nature and function of political theology and it focuses on a number of recent books which either are devoted to the topic or are reflections on Schmitt's book. The second part focuses on the notion of sovereignty, not as a general concept, but as a reflection of Schmitt's concept as set out in *Politische Theologie*. Here, the concern is with a few books but also with articles and chapters. Taken together, these two parts provide an indication of Carl Schmitt's lasting influence on legal philosophy and political thinking. The third part is devoted to allowing Schmitt to have the final word. This is found in his *Politische Theologie II*. Published almost more than a half century after *Politische Theologie*, *Politische Theologie II* provides an intriguing look at how Schmitt's understanding of the connection between law, politics, and theology had changed and what he thought might be some of the lasting ideas from his conception of "political theology."

Keywords Sovereignty today · Political theology today · *Politische Theologie II*

© The Author(s), under exclusive license to Springer Nature
Switzerland AG 2025
C. Adair-Toteff, *Schmitt on Sovereignty and the State of Exception*,
Palgrave Studies in Classical Liberalism,
https://doi.org/10.1007/978-3-031-91728-8_7

While one cannot attribute the interest in sovereignty just to Carl Schmitt, he is the person most responsible for the continuing concern with the notion of political theology. Others before and after him have investigated the nature of sovereignty. But few people before him had thought of a political theology, and it is because of Schmitt that this phrase continues to be used. In effect, Schmitt linked the old notion of sovereignty with his idea of political theology. This linkage should be regarded as one of Carl Schmitt's most important contributions to modern political thought.

This concluding chapter has three parts. The first concerns the continual interest in the nature and function of political theology and it focuses on a number of recent books which either are reflections on Schmitt's book or are devoted to the topic. The second part focuses on the notion of sovereignty, not as a general concept, but as a reflection of Schmitt's concept as set out in *Politische Theologie*. Here, the concern is with a few books but also with articles and chapters. Taken together, these two parts provide an indication of Carl Schmitt's lasting influence on legal philosophy and political thinking. The third part is devoted to allowing Schmitt to have the final word. This is found in his *Politische Theologie II*. Published almost more than a half century after *Politische Theologie*, *Politische Theologie II* provides an intriguing look at how Schmitt's understanding of the connection between law, politics, and theology had changed and what he thought might be some of the lasting ideas from his conception of "political theology."

"POLITICAL THEOLOGY" TODAY

There have been two types of books which focus on the concept of political theology; those which are general accounts and those which specifically respond to Schmitt's books. Examples of the former include the collection edited by Helmut Peukert, and the books by Heinrich Meier and by Paul Kahn. Examples of the latter include the collection edited by W. J. Stankiewicz and the books by Ulrich Haltern and by Wilhelm Hennis. It also includes Helmut Quaritsch's book and especially his 1996 article.

The former volumes include the collection *Diskussion zur "politische Theologie."* This older collection which was edited by Helmut Peukert contained fourteen essays. All of them are worth reading but only if one accepts that the guiding theme of the collection is the relationship between theology and society. Most of these essays had been previously published in theological journals and the ones which had not all focused on the tension between personal religious beliefs and the demands of society. There is less emphasis on politics and far more on theology; and the connections between religion and morality (Peukert, 1969: XI, 38, 132–133, 219, 236–237).

Paul W. Kahn's *Political Theology. Four New Chapters on the Concept of Sovereignty* sounds as if sovereignty is the main focus of this book, but that is slightly misleading. Kahn begins with some correct and even sharp observations about Schmitt's book. Kahn notes that Schmitt's *"Political Theology. Four Chapters on the Concept of Sovereignty* is one of the most famous, as well as one of the most obscure, books in twentieth-century political theory" (Kahn, 2011: 1). He is correct in both claims. Similarly, he is correct when he claims that this fame is based almost exclusively on "just two canonical sentences: 'Sovereign is he who decides on the exception' and 'All significant concepts of the modern theory of the state are secularized theological concepts.'" Kahn's book is not so much a commentary on Schmitt but as his subtitle indicates *New Chapters on the Concept of Sovereignty*. Yet it is a book that tackles a wide range of topics, from law to politics, to philosophy and religion. Scholars mentioned include Aristotle, Edmund Burke, Immanuel Kant, and Hannah Arendt. They also include Hans Kelsen, John Marshall, Ronald Dworkin, and Sonia Sotomayor. They also include Solon, George Soros, Karl Marx, and Osama bin Laden. The concept of sovereignty recedes as notions of authenticity, authority, and causality appear. Sovereignty is obscured by the Counter-Reformation, the Cuban Revolution, and *Bush v Gore*. The Bible and Christianity play a large part in Kahn's book. This is not political theology as much as it is theology masquerading as political theory (Kahn, 2011: 115–119).

Heinrich Meier's *Die Lehre Carl Schmitts. Vier Kapitel zur Unterscheidung Politischer Theologie und Politischer Philosophie* is infused with theological ideas. In contrast to Peukert's collection and Kahn's book, Meier focuses on Schmitt's thinking. It is just not focused on Schmitt's *Politische Theologie*. There are several examples of this: Krabbe and Preuß are not even mentioned and Kelsen warrants only one entry in the index. In contrast, Hegel has twelve entries and Karl Löwith has seven. Plato has ten, Rousseau has eleven. Leo Strauss has more than twenty-five. But it is Hobbes who dominates much of Meier's book. Hobbes is mentioned often, but there are three sections in which he is the focus of Meier's interest (Meier, 1994: 157–175, 180–186, and 194–204). Hobbes is crucial for understanding Schmitt and Meier's interpretation of Hobbes helps illuminate Schmitt's ideas. But some of Meier's interpretation relies on Schmitt's later book on Hobbes; thus, it does not provide much clarification of Schmitt's thinking from his 1922 book. The title of Chapter III is revealing for two reasons: "Offenbarung oder Wer nicht mit mir ist, der ist wider mich." "Offenbarung" ("Revelation") is an indication of the theological dominance in Meier's book and "Who is not with me is against me" is an indication of Schmitt's "friend-enemy" distinction (Meier, 1994: 114–115). It is to Heinrich Meier's credit that he published a book which corrected some of the most glaring misunderstandings of Carl Schmitt's theory of the exception and at the same time clarified some of what Schmitt meant by "political theology." What Meier did not do, was to provide a clarification of what Schmitt meant by "sovereignty."

"Sovereignty" Today

There are a number of books and articles on sovereignty and it is remarkable how often Schmitt is referenced. It is even more remarkable how often his name is missing. A great example of this is *In Defense of Sovereignty*. It is a "symposium" devoted to the importance of sovereignty. It was a "debate" of sorts with one group opposing the use of sovereignty and the other side embracing it (Stankiewicz, 1969: ix–x). It is not really a symposium and not really a debate because the essays were not presented at a conference but were written over a period of more than a decade. Yet, it is a collection of valuable papers devoted to sovereignty. Many of the names listed by Schmitt in *Politische Theologie* are found in this volume: Bodin and Hobbes as well as Krabbe and Preuß—but not Schmitt. Kelsen is not just mentioned often but the collection includes a paper he had published in 1960. "Sovereignty and International Law" may not have been a likely place to see a reference to Schmitt, but Kelsen agreed with Schmitt's claim that sovereignty as a concept has too many meanings (Kelsen, 1969: 115–116).

Schmitt is also missing in the massive volume on sovereignty authored by Helmut Quaritsch. The name Quaritsch surfaces in this chapter three times, first as author, second as editor, and third as author. In 1970 Quaritsch published his "Habilitationschrift" which had the title *Staat und Souveränität*. This volume is just under 600 pages and is a masterful account of the history of sovereignty. Quaritsch began with a brief introduction which was followed by an overview of the concept of the state and the notion of sovereignty. The third chapter was devoted to the Middle Ages while the fourth is a roughly 150-page investigation into Bodin's theory of state and sovereignty (Quaritsch, 1970: 243–394). The fifth chapter is an overview of the theory and practice of sovereignty from Bodin's time until the end of the nineteenth century. Georg Jellinek, Rudolf Smend, and Hermann Heller were mentioned with Jellinek being critically appraised over several pages (Quaritsch, 1970: 22–26). Carl Schmitt was omitted. Anyone one seeking a thorough history of sovereignty should read Quaritsch's book and certainly anyone seeking a thorough investigation of Bodin's concept of sovereignty must consult this book. But to seek Quaritsch's connection to Schmitt, one needs to look at his 1996 essay.

In 1996 Helmut Quaritsch published "Souveränität im Ausnahmezustand. Zum Souveränitätsbegriff im Werk Carl Schmitts." Quaritsch began by indicating his very limited scope; while he contended that Schmitt's ideas about sovereignty were found in *Die Diktatur, Politische Theologie* and *Die Kernfrage des Völkerbundes* (1926), he was focused only on *Die Diktatur* and on the first chapter of *Politische Theologie*. He also noted that Schmitt utilized his ideas about sovereignty to address whatever problem he was confronting: he changed his concept to fit the issue; hence, there is fluidity in Schmitt's concept of sovereignty (Quaritsch, 1996: 1). He spent the first eleven pages on Schmitt's book and the remaining nineteen on Chapter I of *Politische Theologie* (Quaritsch, 1996: 1–11 and 11–30). Quaritsch pointed to three things about the first chapter: first, the opening claim that who decides about the exception is sovereign was announced with fanfare. Second, that Schmitt makes a questionable claim that in Germany between 1871 and 1919, only the state was regarded as sovereign. Third, that Schmitt relies on Bodin but does not mention that Bodin would not have been familiar with the modern "state of exception" ("Ausnahmezustand") (Quaritsch, 1996: 11–15). Quaritsch's further contribution is to connect Schmitt's definition of sovereignty with his book on dictatorship. He had noted the contrast between the 211 footnoted pages of the dictator monograph with the loosely connected four essays that make up his sovereignty collection. Furthermore, *Politische Theologie* was less a work of scholarship than it was an attack on legal positivism (Quaritsch, 1996: 11). He notes further that Schmitt's definition of sovereignty is an ideal typical definition and that it really does not cover the concrete characteristics of the sovereignty of the state. As a result, it is incomplete. Quaritsch notes that

Schmitt is correct in his claim that normal law is not interested in the concept of sovereignty (Quaritsch, 1996: 20–22). That Quaritsch devotes the remaining seven pages to Germany's post war history does nothing to detract from the immense importance in helping to clarify some of the obscure points in Schmitt's concept of sovereignty.

In the 1960s and early 1970s Carl Schmitt was still a persona non grata, but that changed in the 1980s and 1990s. Quaritsch's, 1996 essay was a testament to the fact that Schmitt's politics were often atrocious but his legal thinking should be taken seriously. So, it is perplexing that Schmitt is given little attention in Ulrich Haltern's *Was bedeutet Souveränität*. Published in 2007, Haltern discusses the Catholic concept of sovereignty and notes that it contains the opposition between infinite and finite and suggests "In this sense, sovereignty is always a miracle." ("In diesem Sinne ist Souveränität immer ein Wunder.") (Haltern, 2007: 32). He also investigated the Protestant notion of sovereignty and he begins by indicating that the Protestant Church reduced the importance of authority. He refers to Luther's claim that "The Church is there, where God is." ("Kirche ist da, wo Gott ist.") (Haltern, 2007: 52–53). Haltern discusses Schmitt in relation to Protestantism, which is strange given Schmitt's Catholicism. Haltern makes several references to *Politische Theologie* but they are not always very positive. It appears that Haltern contends that Nazism was an "exception" and since Schmitt was not just the proponent of the "Ausnahme" but endorsed the notion of an unrestricted "will," that Schmitt may have contributed to the rise of Hitler. Haltern decries Schmitt's "Freund-Feind" distinction and seemed to object to Schmitt's claim that all significant legal concepts are secularized theological ones (Haltern, 2007: 10, 55–57).

There are works in which Schmitt's notion of sovereignty does take on a major role. In 1951 Wilhelm Hennis wrote his doctoral dissertation on the problem of sovereignty. His title expressly said that, but his lengthy subtitle indicated that this work was focused both on the modern history of the concept of sovereignty as well as on its contemporary relevance. Hennis would go on to be one of the most astute interpreters of Max Weber's writings and the publishing firm Mohr Siebeck published most of his books. Mohr Siebeck was Weber's publisher and it was responsible for the fifty-volume *Max Weber Gesamtausgabe*. However, Hennis was never a member of the Weber "group" in Germany and he relished his position as an "outsider." Hennis' penetrating analyses of Weber's political thinking are just as rewarding today as they were when he published them. His analysis of the concept of sovereignty is also well worth reading; here the focus is on the second and third chapters.

Hennis' Chapter II began with Stahl and Laband and moved to Jellinek and Anschütz. But the fact that Hennis addressed three of Schmitt's opponents is instructive: Hugo Preuß, Hugo Krabbe, and Hans Kelsen (Hennis, 2003: 14–31). Hennis insisted that Jellinek, Krabbe, and Kelsen stood at the conclusion of an era with the end of the First World War. The revolutionary months of 1918 and the Weimar Constitution were the beginnings of a new era; one which required a different understanding of legal theory in general and sovereignty in particular (Hennis, 2003: 33). He linked Carl Schmitt and Hermann Heller; here only Schmitt will be discussed.

Hennis set the stage by noting that for Kelsen and even Anschütz the question about sovereignty was also about the nature of the state. In this sense, the issue of sovereignty was almost subservient to the matter of the state. In contrast, the issue of sovereignty was of utmost importance to Heller who wrote that it was the crux of the matter. For Hennis, the issue of sovereignty was even more important (Hennis, 2003: 34–35).

Hennis began the section on Carl Schmitt with the famous introductory sentence "Souverän ist, wer über den Ausnahmezustand entscheidet." He noted that it was found in the 1922 edition of *Politische Theologie* and that he carried it over to the 1934 edition. Hennis insisted that it was fundamental to Schmitt's decisionism and that it has lost none of its power. He also insisted that this was Schmitt's response to the increasing emphasis on pluralism which Schmitt contended was undermining the unity of the state. Hennis claimed that the notion of the need for the state's unity was Schmitt's fundamental preoccupation from 1922 until 1932. Hennis further emphasized how crucial the "state of exception" ("Ausnahmezustand") was for Schmitt. Norms were applicable to normal cases, but norms were not applicable to chaos. That which is normally regarded as useful, purposeful, and substantial is irrelevant for the abnormal. In a telling phrase Hennis equates "the case of exception" with the "case of sovereignty" ("Im Ausnahmefall, d.h. Souveränitätfall"); thus, only the decider determines because the norms have no jurisdiction in such cases. This led Hennis to complain that Schmitt's sovereign is really nothing more than an "uncontrolled arbitrary will." It is uncontrolled because no one can hinder this will; it is arbitrary because it does not believe in the need for justification. Hennis further complains that rather than following Bodin's notion of sovereignty, Schmitt was promoting dictatorship (Hennis, 2003: 41–44). It was at this point that Hennis stopped focusing on *Politische Theology* and began to consider Schmitt's later writings. Hennis' *Das Problem der Souveränität* is one of the clearest and most penetrating analyses of the concept of sovereignty as well as containing a short but exceptionally acute account of Schmitt's notion of sovereignty. If the writings on political theology emphasized theology, the writings on sovereignty emphasized its conceptual history. Meier's book is worth reading and, Hennis' posthumously book even more so, but it is Quaritsch's essay that is the most informative and therefore requires reading.

CARL SCHMITT'S "SOVEREIGN THEOLOGY"

The first edition of *Politische Theologie* remained unaltered for the second edition. Writing in December 1933 Carl Schmitt insisted that the work had stood the test of time and that his indictment of liberal normativism was still strikingly relevant. He left it open whether there is there should be a political theology or an unpolitical theology. Schmitt did indicate an expansion of his ideas as found in the book from 1922. The first was an indication that he no longer believed in two types of legal thinking. Besides the liberal's normative and his own decisionism, he contended that there was third type which was an institutional science of law. The other shift is shown by a new trinity: "state, movement, people" ("Staat, Bewegung, Volk") (Schmitt, 1934: 7–8, 2015: 7–9). Schmitt did not expand upon these points.

In 1970 Schmitt published *Politische Theologie II*. This title suggests that this book is a continuation or a revisiting the theses that he had laid out in the book from 1922. There are certain themes that are repeated: his claim that legal positivists reject any and all indications of theology or metaphysics as being untenable in juridical writings (Schmitt, 1970: 12). He also maintained that he began his investigations into the meaning of sovereignty with *Die Diktatur* and he clarifies that his concept of the political first appeared as an article in the *Archiv für Sozialwissenschaft und Sozialpolitik* in 1927. He reminded his readers that "Der Begriff des Politischen" began with the sentence "The concept of the state presupposes the concept of the political." ("Der Begriff des Staates setzt den Begriff des Politischen voraus.") And, he reminded them that his systematic work was a "doctrine of the *Constitution*" ("*Verfassung*slehre") and not a "doctrine of the *State*" ("*Staat*slehre") (Schmitt, 1970: 25). But much of *Politische Theologie II* is taken up with Schmitt's conflicts with other scholars. In particular, he addressed a number of works by the theologian Erik Peterson. Schmitt disagreed with Peterson's use of the phrase "political theology," but agreed with Edward Caird that "metaphysics is the most intensive and clearest expression of an age" (Schmitt, 1970: 56). Schmitt also complained that Peterson did not see the connection between metaphysics and theology, and he appeared to have ignored the relationship between law and theology. In this, Schmitt praised the legal theorist and Protestant Church historian Rudolph Sohm for seeing this connection so clearly (Schmitt, 1970: 99–101). Schmitt concluded *Politische Theologie II* with some revealing comments. He contrasted "stasis" with "kinesis"; the first signifies rest, peace, and status, and the second signifies its opposite, lack of rest, movement, and even civil war. Given Schmitt's emphasis on movement and lack of peace, it is no wonder that he thought that politics belonged to "kinesisi." Another revealing comment was his contrast between the world-rejecting God of love and the worldly God of justice. Just as there is the opposition of the "creator God" ("Schöpfergott") and the "savior God" ("Erlösergott") there is also the opposition between lightness and darkness (Schmitt, 1970: 117–120). Schmitt sought to place these dualisms in a value-neutral light; but, it was evident which side he seemed to think was better and that was the side with the most power—not political *theology*, but *political* theology.

It is worth recalling Carl Schmitt's musings from the months of confinement. He did not list any of his constitutional opponents like Kelsen, Anschütz, or Heller. Nor did he mention his constitutional friends like Grau and Smend. Instead, Schmitt claimed that not only was he indebted to Bodin and Hobbes, but that he felt a close kinship with them. If that was not clear enough, he insisted that Bodin and Hobbes had stood at the beginning of the era of the doctrine of the state and that he stood at the closing end of the "Staatslehre." (Schmitt, 1950: 63, 66, 72–7, 63–64, 67, 72–75). It is in this context that one should consider the two passages that Kahn had mentioned and the one that Haltern had also alluded to. Haltern had also mentioned Schmitt's "Freund-Feind" distinction. Ernst-Wolfgang Böckenförde presented his paper "Der Begriff des Politischen als Schlüssel zum Staatsrechtlichen Werk Carl Schmitts" in which he claimed that Schmitt's book on the concept of the political was the key to understanding Schmitt's legal thinking. He pointed specifically to the "Freund-Feind" distinction because it was one important means to ensure national unity (Böckenförde, 1988: 284,

298–299, 302). That paper was first published in the collection edited by Helmut Quaritsch and it caused considerable discussion (Quaritsch, 1988: 301–303, 313–315). However, Böckenförde also cited Schmitt's claim that the sovereign is the one who decides the exception (Böckenförde, 1988: 287). There is no question that much of Schmitt's reputation rests on the "Freund-Feind" distinction from *Der Begriff des Politischen* but I will suggest that the key to understanding Schmitt's legal theory is found in *Politische Theologie*. It is there that Schmitt states his approach to law the most clearly and that what is important is not the normal but the abnormal. That is why he assigns the title of sovereign to the one who decides: "Souverän ist, wer über den Ausnahmezustand entscheidet." That sentence began Schmitt's *Politische Theologie* but it introduces what might be called his "sovereign theology."

REFERENCES

Böckenförde, E.-W. (1988). Der Begriff des Politischen als Schlüssel zum staatrechtlichen Werk Carl Schmitts. *In Quaritsch, 1988*, 283–299.

Haltern, U. (2007). *Was bedeutet Souveränität?* Mohr Siebeck.

Hennis, W. (2003). *Das Problem der Souveränität. Ein Beitrag zur neuren Literaturgeschichte und gegenwärtigen Problematik der politischen Wissenschaften* (1951). Mit einem Vorwort von Christian Starck. Mohr Siebeck.

Kahn, D. (2011). *Political Theology. Four New Chapters on the Concept of Sovereignty*. Columbia University Press.

Kelsen, H. (1969). Sovereignty and International Law. In Stankiewicz 115–131.

Meier, H. (1994). *Die Lehre Carl Schmitts. Vier Kapitel zur Untersuchung Politischer Theologie und Politischer Philosophie*. Verlag J.B. Metzler.

Peukert, H., Hrsg. (1969). *Diskussion zur "politische Theologie."* Matthias-Grünewald-Verlag. Chr. Kaiser Verlag.

Quaritsch, H. (1996). Souveränität im Ausnahmezustand. Zum Souveränitätsbegriff im Werk Carl Schmitts. In *Der Staat. Zeitschrift für Staatslehre Öffentliches Recht und Verfassungsgeschichte* (Vol. 35, pp. 1–30). Band Heft 1/4.

Quaritsch, H. (Ed.). (1988). *Complexio Oppositorum. Über Carl Schmitt*. Duncker & Humblot.

Quaritsch, H. (1970). *Staat und Souveränität. Band 1: Die Grundlagen*. Athenäum Verlag.

Schmitt, C. (2015). *Politische Theologie*. Duncker & Humblot. Zehnte Auflage.

Schmitt, C. (1970). *Politische Theologie II. Die Legende von der Erledigung jeder Politischen Theologie*. Duncker & Humblot.

Schmitt, C. (1950). *Ex Captivitate Salus*. Greven Verlag.

Schmitt, C. (1934). *Politische Theologie*. Duncker & Humblot.
Schmitt, C. (1923). Soziologie des Souveränitätsbegriffes und politische Theologie. In *Hauptprobleme der Soziologie. Erinnerungsgabe für Max Weber* (pp. 4–35). Herausgegeben von Melchior Palyi. Verlag von Duncker & Humblot.
Stankiewicz, W. J. (Ed.). (1969). *In Defense of Sovereignty*. Oxford University Press.

The manufacturer's authorised representative in the EU is Springer Nature Customer Service Centre GmbH, Europaplatz 3, 69115 Heidelberg, Germany. If you have any concerns regarding our products, please contact ProductSafety@springernature.com

Printed and bound by CPI Group (UK) Ltd, Croydon, CR0 4YY

28/04/2026

02098473-0001